WHY CAN'T MY GARDEN LOOK LIKE THAT?

More gardening books from Spring Hill

Planting Plans for Your Kitchen Garden

How to create a vegetable, herb and fruit garden in easy stages

Holly Farrell

Use the easy-to-follow planting plans in this book to turn your back garden or allotment into a productive paradise.

Paperback: 978-1-908974-02-0   £14.99

The Little Book of Popular Perennials

A guide to the selection and cultivation of your favourite plants

Maureen Little

A beautifully illustrated portable reference text on all aspects of growing – and caring for your favourite perennials.

Paperback: 978-1-908974-90-0   £9.99

Write or phone for a catalogue to:

How To Books
Spring Hill House, Spring Hill Road, Begbroke, Oxford OX5 1RX
Tel. 01865 375794
Or email: info@howtobooks.co.uk

Visit our website www.howtobooks.co.uk to find out more about us and our books.

Like our Facebook page **How To Books & Spring Hill**
Follow us on **Twitter @Howtobooksltd**
Read our books online www.howto.co.uk

WHY CAN'T MY GARDEN LOOK LIKE THAT?

Proven, Easy Ways to Make a Beautiful Garden of Your Own

JOHN SHORTLAND

SPRING HILL

Constable & Robinson Ltd
55–56 Russell Square
London WC1B 4HP
www.constablerobinson.com

First published in the UK by Spring Hill,
an imprint of Constable & Robinson Ltd, 2013

A copy of the British Library Cataloguing in
Publication Data is available from the British Library

ISBN 978-1-908974-10-5

Designed by Ian Hughes, Mousemat Design Limited

Printed and bound in Spain

1 3 5 7 9 10 8 6 4 2

Contents

Foreword

I feel botanically linked to John Shortland, the author of this enticing book. In the late 19th century my great-grandfather, a passionate gardener, re-designed the grounds of his house, Kiddington Hall, in Oxfordshire, and planted some exceptional trees. As a child, when my grandfather was living there, I loved playing under those majestic trees, and made friends with the gardener, Mr Faint. Almost fifty years later it was John Shortland, author of this book, who kept the Kiddington gardens beautiful, so the pleasure of them is what we share.

Why Can't My Garden Look Like That? includes everything you need to know, from the practical to the creative. It is like having a friend to whom you can always turn for un-daunting advice. Whether you're new to gardening or have been digging, planting, pruning and tending for years, this book will inspire you. You will want to plan a new garden, or re-think an old one; concentrate more on contrasting size, shape and colour; look after your old favourites better and try out new varieties. And before long, on a brilliant early summer's day, someone will say to you 'Why can't my garden look like yours?'

Josceline Dimbleby

Introduction

There are many reasons why we garden but, more often than not, the one that started us off is simply that a garden came attached to the first house we were responsible for. Perhaps the previous owners had been keen gardeners and, over time, you have watched overwhelmed as it steadily went downhill. Or perhaps your house is new and the builders have laid grass and randomly planted a tree and a few odd shrubs to enhance an otherwise stark appearance.

Of course, sometimes it is none of these things: you've worked hard over the years but the garden has simply not quite done what you had hoped for or it has outgrown its allotted space. Everywhere you look – in glossy magazines or when visiting National Trust properties or even friends' houses – you see your ideal and hear yourself exclaiming 'Why can't mine look like that?' The simple answer is it can; you don't need to be an 'expert' and more often than not it can be done with surprisingly little effort.

You don't need to be an 'expert' to have a beautiful garden – there are simple techniques that can have immediate effect

To have a stunning garden you need to answer some questions truthfully for it can be surprisingly hard, sometimes, to view something you badly want dispassionately. The most important question of all is 'Do I like gardening?' If the answer has a 'but' in it those are the first issues to address – write them down. So for example, if the response is 'Yes, but it is difficult to find the time' then this is most likely the key to all the on-going problems. The good news is that it is quite possible to have a great garden without spending every spare hour in it.

Time, of course, is the major factor. If you are only free at weekends and you have to juggle those hours to fit in child dance and music lessons, dog walking and doing the washing and ironing, it is necessary to allow for that in the garden plan of action. If time is at a premium it is far better to have a simple yet beautiful garden to maintain than to have a complicated one that is a constant heartache. Simple does not have to mean boring. There are always opportunities for expanding the gardening activities as your circumstances change and you become confident that you are able to cope with its increased demands. Likewise, if you find yourself with less time to devote to it, it is better to reduce the number of tasks required than to struggle on and feel constantly dissatisfied. Gardening should always be a pleasure — it is important to remember that.

The weather also plays a great part in gardening and not just in the obvious way of the sun and rain requirements of plants. Are you a fair weather gardener or are you the sort of person that likes to be outside regardless of the climate? All of these things have to be written down on the list and taken into account. There are no right or wrong answers for we are all different.

So far we have assumed that you do like working in the garden even if, at times, it all gets a bit much. If you don't especially enjoy it but want a nice garden there are still ways to approach it and once you start to see results you will almost certainly begin to like doing it more. Gardening can be as addictive as any drug — once you've been on a 'high' with it you will want to be there over and over again.

Write a list with all the issues that have stopped you from having the garden you want on one side. On the other, list all the tasks that you enjoy — as well as those that you don't.

Giving honest thought now to how you feel about gardening and just how much time you are able to devote to it is the first stage to success. The next is to be equally critical of the layout of the garden. This process is covered in detail in Chapter 1 and is quite straightforward. You do not have to be able to draw, although it can be helpful — it is perfectly possible to make your design directly on the ground with nothing more than a hosepipe and can of spray paint. However you approach it, by the end of the review you will have decided upon the basic layout of the garden, even if in conclusion it remains unchanged.

Using a hosepipe to mark out a design

It is often said that the definition of a weed is a plant growing in the wrong place and this is equally true of garden plants. There has to be a very good reason for keeping one that you dislike; don't be afraid to get rid of it. Remember, also, that just one half-dead plant can completely destroy the appearance of the garden and you have to learn to be ruthless if your garden is always to look its best. Sometimes the different plants are nice enough but are grouped badly or there just aren't enough of them: all of these things can be rectified. Make a note of those that you want to keep and those that need to go – if you don't know the names of the plants you can always take photos. The Latin names of plants often strike terror into the heart of even the most enthusiastic gardener for we have all met those that take delight in showing off their knowledge at every available moment, regardless of the fact that they are obviously boring everyone to death.

You don't need to learn the Latin names of plants, although you probably already know more than you think. Iris and dahlia are just two examples.

When we are striving for the garden of our dreams we need to look beyond the individual plants for, although some plants look good in isolation, the majority don't. It is also necessary to think beyond flower colour (for this is often fleeting) and to look at the texture and colour of their leaves and stems as well.

Imagine, for a moment, a woman wearing an all green outfit: a pale green jacket worn over a pale green blouse and matched with a pale green skirt along with accessories. Stockings, shoes, handbags, jewellery and hat are all in the same uniform shade and material. However beautiful she might be, or gorgeous the colour, the effect will be dull. But take the same outfit and mix the fabrics so that the blouse is silky and the jacket and skirt crepe. Make the accessories a tone or two darker and suddenly the outfit is transformed. It is still green but heads are turned in admiration. The same applies to the garden, for it is quite possible to have a beautiful garden which is all green and, once this is realised, flower colour becomes an added bonus.

It is very simple to change the plants in the garden and to create new design features but the two things that are difficult to alter are its aspect and soil type. Certain plants require quite specific conditions to thrive and it is pointless trying to grow, say rhododendrons, if you don't have the right soil. For the best results always work with what you have got, don't fight with nature for you are only likely to lose, although this doesn't mean you can't improve what you have.

Let us assume that you have now carried out many of the recommendations in this book and are now reasonably content with the appearance of the garden. I use the word 'reasonably' with intent, for a gardener is rarely completely satisfied as new ideas always come to mind as enthusiasm and knowledge is gained. This is how it should be for a great garden evolves steadily and rarely remains unchanged. In Chapter 6 we look at maintenance issues as without regular weeding and tidying the garden will soon deteriorate again. This will give you no cause for concern for you will have adjusted the garden to give you plenty of time to maintain it without too much angst, especially if you have the right tools for the job.

You don't need lots of different tools and expensive equipment, just a few well chosen ones.

Pruning is another task many gardeners shy away from, resulting in a plant that becomes ever larger. In desperation it is totally removed or chopped about, often leaving a very unattractive plant. Pruning manuals can seem very complicated to follow and what happens if you don't know the name of the plant anyway? Actually, it doesn't matter that much for there are straightforward techniques to guide you and by following these you can create a good looking plant that is healthy as well as keeping it within its allotted space.

Gardening should be an adventure – a voyage of discovery – for no two gardens are alike and nor are their problems or solutions. By following the techniques and advice given in this book it is hoped that even the most reluctant gardener will become an adventurer, exploring the delights and issues of their own garden and experimenting with every challenge that they produce. Your eyes and an enquiring mind are the most valuable tools that you can have in a garden and by constantly questioning 'why?' or, even better, 'why not?' your garden will respond generously. If the solution suits you and your plot then you can be quite certain that you have come across the right answer and you will achieve the garden of your dreams.

CHAPTER ONE

Getting Started

Reviewing what you already have

Even if you are content with the layout of your garden and only want to alter the planting, it is still a good idea to review the whole garden periodically. You may discover the need to make a few adjustments and it is far better to do this now than to disturb new plantings as they are becoming established. Do get into the habit of writing down or drawing your ideas.

For a new garden or one that requires change, the review process helps you analyse any issues and requirements that you may have and helps you avoid making costly errors.

Get snapping: taking photographs

Before you even consider what needs to be done with the garden the first task is to photograph it. You don't need to be a David Bailey, just snap away. First of all, take photos from every window of the house, followed by various shots from around the garden including looking back at the house itself. Make sure that you also include individual or groups of plants that you like and also those that you do not. These photos will all become a reminder of how the garden used to look. Later, you will also find them useful with the review process and with forward planning. Once this is done it is time to take a long, hard look at the garden itself.

Take lots of photos before, during and after you start making alterations. They will become morale-boosting reminders of just how far you have progressed.

Choosing the right place for your paths and patios

If you think of your garden as a living body — and I don't just mean the plants, animals and insects that dwell in it — the paths, patios and borders are its skeleton. These are the 'bones' upon which all else depends and it is essential that time is spent getting them right.

Paths

Paths are the routes that we take when we walk around the garden. An obvious statement perhaps, but are the existing ones in the right place and where do they need to take you? A shortcut across a lawn is still a path even if it is an invisible one. If, as often becomes the case, it is visible as worn, sparse grass or, even worse, a muddy track, it most certainly needs to be rethought. A path in everyday use needs to be practical which usually means straight or with a gentle curve. These paths take you briskly along them whereas a less frequently used one can be meandering, allowing a more leisurely pace.

The place to start considering where they should be sited is by the most frequently used garden door whether this is a kitchen, conservatory, French door or side entrance. It is often easier to view from an upstairs window, for looking down upon the garden it appears as a map waiting to have its 'roads' drawn onto it.

Paths in regular use are best made using a hard-wearing material such as stone or gravel; grass is perfectly adequate, as well as pleasing to the eye, for wandering between borders. The width of the path is perhaps even more important as every path, whatever its purpose, must be of comfortable proportions. No path wants to be less than 60cm wide and 90–120cm, if space permits, is better by far and, of course, not all

A formal path's appearance can be softened by lush planting

paths in the garden need to be the same width.

Paths can be used to deceive the eye by leading nowhere, for with clever planting they can appear to be taking you to an unseen part of a non-existent garden, a ploy often used in smaller ones. In larger gardens, paths can lead you to areas of different character.

Patios and terraces

Despite the vagaries of the British climate, most gardens require a place to sit. A patio or terrace needs to be large enough to entertain your family and friends: make sure there is space for a table and chairs, perhaps a barbecue, and that there is still room to move around comfortably. Whereabouts does it need to be sited? Close to the back of the house is the usual place for both privacy and convenience, but if this is in shade at the time you are most likely to use it consider placing it in a sunnier spot. If you like having a morning coffee or breakfast outdoors remember that the sun will be shining elsewhere; there is no reason why you cannot have two dining areas.

Barbecues

People tend to fall into two categories – those that barbecue and those that don't. Barbecuing is a very social activity and the barbecue, whether built in or free standing, needs to be positioned with some thought. It needs to be far enough away and downwind so that your guests are not smoked out (remember, also, smoke drift into neighbours), yet close enough for the chef and the cooking to be part of the entertainment. One way to achieve this is to position the barbecue on a 'spur' off the main area.

Garden seating

It is also pleasant having other places to sit in the garden. Benches give out the message 'come and join me', whereas individual chairs say quite the opposite. Either way it is nice, perhaps essential, to make a place for a glass of chilled, white wine to be put down safely.

A strategically placed seat can become a focal point in the garden or, if more tucked away, somewhere you can enjoy a quiet moment.

Positioning your beds and borders

Now that you have a firm idea where the path and seating areas are to be it is time to review the shape of the beds and borders. It is important when doing this not to be too influenced by what is already growing in them unless you are certain that trees or larger shrubs are to remain. Even then, there is nothing that cannot make a tree at present situated in a border become one that is surrounded by, say, grass – or vice versa. Smaller shrubs and other plants, on the other hand, can generally be moved so do not need to be taken into consideration. Why are some planted areas called beds while others are called borders? As with most things, ask two people the same question and you are likely to get two different answers. A bed can be defined either as a smallish area often formally layed out or one that is raised above the surrounding ground level. A border tends to be larger and more informally planted with a mix of all sorts of different plants. In reality there is no difference: both are cultivated areas devoted to the growing of plants.

The place to start this review is, once again, from inside the house for this is where you will see the garden most of the time.

Blue and white border

Once you have a clear idea of where your paths and seating areas are to be placed, the positioning and shape of your borders tend to become more obvious.

Formal or informal style?

You will probably already know if you prefer a formal or informal style, but just because you have chosen a straight line for your path doesn't mean that you have to do the same for your borders. A temptation when choosing the informal style is to have far too many curves. Not only do they never look as good as when there are fewer, they make grass cutting a chore and, however much time you are prepared to spend labouring in the garden, you don't want to waste precious moments on that sort of work. Likewise with a formal style: sharp, right-angled corners can look fabulous but mowing them well is tricky and nothing looks worse than scalped, bald patches of lawn because the mower keeps slipping over the edge. This can be avoided by rounding off the corners so that the mower will glide effortlessly around them, saving you valuable time and frayed tempers.

Shade

As with the patio, some borders will be shadier than others depending on where you place them. It is better to ensure that the borders are correctly sited to please the eye and then worry about the aspect. There are times when this cannot be the case – heavy shade severely limits your choice of plants, north or east-facing borders to a lesser extent. If having plenty of flowers is really important then they need to be accommodated where they will flourish in the sunnier parts of the garden.

Hedges, fences and walls

It is often tempting to place borders along boundaries and if these are in front of a hedge then maintenance, roots and the lowering of nutrients and soil moisture can all be problems. Despite this, a neatly clipped hedge can make a lovely backdrop to the flower border, but do allow space for positioning of ladders and the fallen clippings that will need to be raked up and cleared. Allow room in front of the hedge for this and time will be saved and your plants prevented from getting damaged. Grassing this strip over also saves you time, for it is then easy to keep tidy by running over it with a mower, as well as providing clean access for border maintenance in wet weather – it also gives you an additional path.

Leaving space to work in between the hedge and the back of a border makes cutting and clearing very much quicker and easier.

Consider, too, what height you want your hedge to be and whether it should retain its leaves through the winter. With either choice, a hedge will be a dominant feature of your garden at all times of the year so its position and its overall balance within the design must be thought about.

A wall or a fence makes a useful additional growing space for climbers. Remember, too, that not all borders have to run along the boundaries for, sometimes, all this does is to visually reinforce the perimeter of a garden.

Borders can be of any shape and size and in any position, but the secret

The informal planting of this huge border softens its more formal shape

to having a stunning garden is to ensure that your planted areas are large enough to have impact.

Do avoid having too many small or narrow beds.

Take more photographs and keep writing

Unless you are blessed with great memory it is sensible to continue writing down all your ideas for future reference. It isn't necessary to have great drawing skills as all you are trying to do is to place the major features of the garden onto paper. On garden plans the north position is always shown: add it if you wish. A more useful form of the same information is just to hatch over the areas that are in shade for the greater part of the day as this will act as a reminder when deciding on which plants to put where.

Earlier, we talked about taking photographs and these are very helpful at this stage. Experiment by drawing your different ideas over them and see which look the best but remember that you are only looking at the overall shapes in the garden and whether they look balanced and pleasing to the eye; what you fill the borders with, whether it is with shrubs, flowers, bulbs or a mix of them all, comes later.

Print your photographs on ordinary paper in black and white as colours can be a distraction.

Do you need a lawn?

The majority of gardeners prefer to have an expanse of lawn and an area of finely cut grass does offset a garden beautifully. When well maintained it can offer a soothing, cool and fresh look on a hot summer's day or a playground for the children. In winter, it provides welcome greenery to a drab landscape – although, of course, your garden will, unlike many others, still have interest then too. A good-looking lawn, however, comes at a price: it needs to be regularly mown, its edges kept trimmed and it should not have many weeds, all of which are time consuming to achieve. Ignore this and you will never have a great garden however clever you are with design or with plants. Tempting though it may be, removing the grass and replacing it with something else isn't necessarily going to help. Gravel is often described as an easy, low maintenance alternative but this isn't strictly true for reasons discussed on page 152.

If you have been following the suggestions above, the size and shape of the lawn will have formed naturally as you positioned the paths, patios and borders – the areas you have left become grass but, as always, with some provisos.

Lawns, like flower beds, tend to look more impressive the larger they are.

Very small patches of grass can appear out of place and are nearly always a nuisance to mow and care for: consider doing away with them altogether. Paving, gravel or even planting up the whole garden are different options. Grass also does not grow well in heavy shade and if you have an area like that you can experiment and see if it grows to an acceptable standard, perhaps by not mowing it as frequently. An alternative would be to treat it differently perhaps by laying a circle of granite setts beneath a tree; these cope with movement by tree roots whereas a slab would, in time, lift or crack. A cheaper alternative would be to spread bark chips or gravel beneath it but these would be more difficult and time consuming to keep clear of fallen leaves and debris.

There are solutions to every issue in your garden but the consequences do need to be thought about to see if there are ways of simplifying the on-going maintenance.

In larger gardens, allowing some grass to grow longer is a great way to give additional interest and to cut down on the maintenance. It can still be mown regularly on a much higher blade setting than normal to maintain a degree of formality or mown less often for a more natural look. If you choose the latter option the grass will still need attention but it tends to be at a time when there is less to do elsewhere.

The contrasting textures of formal lawn and wild flower meadow creates additional interest as well as cutting down on mowing

Growing your own vegetables and herbs

Vegetable growing is becoming increasingly popular once again and it is possible to grow some of them within the flower borders if you haven't much room. If you want to include crops that need to be dug up when harvesting such as potatoes or carrots they do need to be grown in a separate designated area. Careful thought needs to be given to this for not only do they require adequate sunlight to thrive, maintenance can also be an issue – do you have the time and energy to devote to them? Nothing looks more depressing than a weed-infested expanse of vegetable garden in winter with nothing to show other than a few leeks and mouldering cabbages. One way is to hide it behind a low hedge of some kind or to make it a design feature in its own right, splitting the area up into smaller, more manageable beds.

Herbs are best placed as close to the kitchen as possible for no-one wants to make a dash to a far corner of the garden for a sprig of thyme or parsley halfway through the cooking process.

Herbs can be grown in a very small space or in pots or, as most of them are quite decorative, at the front of the flower border.

A mass of herbs growing on a kitchen windowsill

Washing lines, dustbins and trampolines

These feature in a garden usually more prominently than we would care for. Thinking through their position at this stage means they can often be placed more discreetly, although in the case of trampolines their size makes them difficult. If the users are small children then it needs to be sited nearby so that their safety can be monitored. Thinking longer term, as they become older will it be possible to move it to a more out of the way place? Work this into the equation now and the garden will not have to be altered too much at a later date.

Washing lines also need to be near to the house and away from trees and shrubs for practical reasons. The sight of an unused rotary line standing proudly as the centrepiece of a garden is all too common; bring them out only on washing days and store them the rest of the time, especially when you are wanting to show off the garden to friends.

Dustbins can often be hidden by carefully planted shrubs or by trellis or other fencing for they need to be close to the house and easily reached by a good path.

What to do with your garden rubbish

Finally, what are you planning to do with all the weeds, lawn clippings and fallen leaves that you will accumulate? Most, if not all, councils now have a regular garden waste collection and this is one option for disposal, as is taking it yourself to your local tip. A much better option is to home compost. Plastic composting bins are readily available or it is quite easy to make your own timber bins (see page 106). Smaller gardens probably only require one bin but in larger ones it is often convenient to have two or more, one close to the house, the others further away wherever the bulk of the waste originates. Rats, incidentally, are rarely a problem with well managed composting.

Whenever you can, carry out home composting; the resulting product is full of nutrients to feed your garden and, best of all, it is free.

Congratulate yourself!

Now that you have completed the review process you have – whether you have it mapped out on paper or not (and, again I would urge you to do so) – a new plan for your garden. However delighted you are at your achievement it is important to remember that it is only there as a guide. A common mistake is to think that it cannot be adjusted if it should prove necessary and there is no need to feel that somehow the design is not good or you have failed in some way. The sole purpose of everything you have done so far is to create a great garden and if that means, say, moving a path a few feet to the right to perfect it, where's the big deal in that? You have created a blueprint or map that will become the most important document you have, one that you will refer to time and time again.

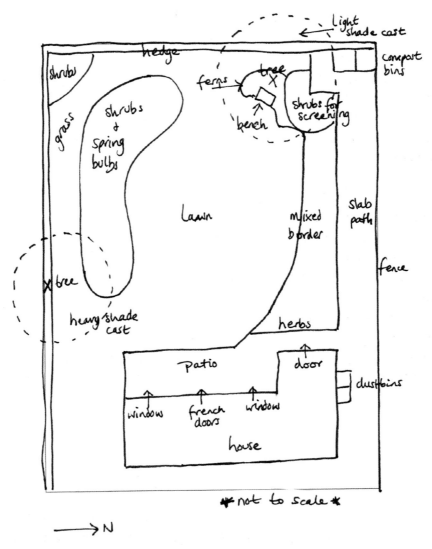

A rough sketch for a back garden plan

How to turn your ideas into reality

So, looking at the paper in front of you, how do you know that it is going to make a great garden? The secret is not to dive in with fork and spade but to 'draw' it out on the ground first. If you are the meticulous sort then, by all means, use tape measures to get total accuracy but even if you can't be bothered with that it is wise to be as thorough as you can. Remember the skeleton analogy? Just as in humans, the 'flesh' (plants) can be added to or removed relatively easily whereas breaking the 'bones' once they are set will require more lengthy, and quite probably painful, surgery.

Marking out your garden plan

Marking out is actually quite easy. All that is required is some string, a few bamboo canes and a spray can of road paint which is readily available from a builder's merchant.

Marking out the garden is an exciting process as you will see your ideas suddenly spring to life. Don't be afraid to adjust the layout if necessary to achieve the look you want.

Just as in the initial process, start with the main paths and patio, marking them out if straight with string stretched taut between two bamboo pegs. If you have decided to have curves it is easier to use a garden hosepipe or a thicker rope to mark the shape as these can be adjusted more easily. For making circles place a peg at its centre, tie a length of string to the spray can and attach the other end to the peg. Now, keeping the string stretched taut, walk slowly around spraying directly onto the ground and the circle appears before your eyes. Don't forget that whatever diameter you want your circle to be the length of the string will need to be half that size.

When planning to lay paving slabs or blocks it is sensible to measure the width accurately to avoid having to make too many cuts of the stone – as these can be bought in a number of different sizes it isn't difficult to end up with the desired width. Where paths are to be of mown grass measure the width of your mower's cut and multiply these to get the size you want for there is nothing more irritating or time consuming than having to cut a narrow strip of grass to complete the job.

You may prefer to mark out all of the paths and any patios with strings first for, although this can result sometimes in rather a lot of lines and pegs, an obvious error can then be quickly adjusted. Once this is completed it is time to spray paint along all of the string lines which can then be removed. Stand back and look, for you now have your paths and seating areas laid out before you. Take time to walk up and down them, even place your garden furniture if you wish to make sure that they are of the correct size. How do they feel? How do they look? If content, it is then time to follow the procedure again, this time marking out the garden borders and other planted areas. You can, of course, always do this with different coloured paint. Once again stand back and look at the garden from all angles and make any further adjustments, if necessary, by rubbing out the paint lines with your foot and spraying again.

The process is now complete. Despite any misgivings that you might have had when you started, you have in front of you a garden design and one that you can proudly claim as your own.

Front gardens

Regardless of the weather or the time of year front gardens are used every day and need to always look good. They should be kept as simple in design and planting as possible for who wants to spend more time than necessary maintaining them?

The design springs to life once it is physically marked out in the garden

CHAPTER TWO

Looking Good Throughout the Year

Before we rush off to the garden centre or start planting we need to give some thought as to how our garden can look good whatever the season. It is relatively easy to have a floriferous spring and early summer garden but as the year progresses will the garden still be head turning?

If you receive compliments on a bleak winter's day it confirms that you have created a great garden.

To achieve this it is important to have a good mix of plants although this does not necessarily mean that you need dozens of different varieties – some of the best gardens limit their plant selection to just a few carefully chosen ones, relying upon repetition for impact. Unless you are restricted to a very small space, it is possible to have different areas of the garden peaking at different times of the year. Sometimes it is essential to do this if, for example, part of it is in dry, heavy shade through the summer months: this could be the place to have a fine display of spring bulbs, leaving the rest of the garden to outshine it through the remainder of the year.

A garden can still look beautiful during the winter months

How to create visual interest

Leaves

Remember the analogy of the lady wearing green? If the clever use of foliage can make the garden look great just think of the potential when it comes to adding flower colour too. There are a number of factors to consider when thinking leaves: colour – for they aren't just in differing shades of green, there are also purples, silver-greys and golds as well as variegated combinations; texture – which can be coarse, smooth, soft or lacy. They also come in many sizes and shapes – ranging from tiny to huge; palm shaped to grassy and sword-like. This may sound terribly complicated but as in every other aspect of gardening there are simple rules that help you bypass the tricky bits.

When it comes to thinking leaves, the basic rule is, once again, to mix and match. For example, break up the dense, small-leafed shrub with something more open growing and with a larger leaf; if the overall effect looks too green add some plants of a different leaf colour.

There are, of course, two other important aspects to consider when making choices about leaves. First of all, does the plant keep its leaves during the winter ('evergreens') or do they lose them ('deciduous')? If the latter, do they have good autumn colour, by which we mean do the leaves turn gold,

Leaves come in many different guises – the grey-green needles of this pine give all-year interest

crimson or yellow before dropping? A fine autumn display is a very exciting sight and one that many people focus on when selecting plants, but it is well to remember that, in the majority of years, the spectacle is quite fleeting, sometimes lasting just a matter of days. I recommend not planting specifically for this – just consider it a bonus if you get it – however, this doesn't mean you can't think about it when planning.

Evergreens are quite a different prospect. There should be a good number of plants that continue to offer something during the winter months although it can be tempting to add too many to a garden. If too few it is easy for them to look isolated once all the other plants have become dormant; when overdone, they can appear oppressive and dark.

It is usually better if you plant evergreens in groups. This will give them heightened importance as well as balance during the winter months.

Bark and stems

It isn't only leaves that offer winter interest: the bark and stem colour of a number of shrubs and trees can add greatly to the appearance of the garden. Unlike leaves, however, the majority of these are grown specifically for this purpose and do not have a major role to play during other seasons, although this does not mean that they aren't attractive then, they are just outshone by other plants. They are best planted in specific places where they can create a focal point.

The extraordinary bark of myrtle requires a sheltered spot to develop to its full glory

The shape (form) of plants

Now that we have considered texture, we need to think about the form of the plant, by which we mean shape. This isn't too difficult either for the principles are the same as selecting leaves: if the plant grows tall and upright consider placing it beside one that is arching or spreading. Once you begin to play around with shape in your head or on paper it becomes ever easier, especially if you think of the shape of the plant at its most basic: round, oblong, triangular. Most garden centre purchased plants come with labels that will tell you, amongst other things, just what shape it will grow into as well as its ultimate height and spread and this will guide you if you are unsure.

Shape can be dramatically altered by the pruning and clipping of hedges or shrubs.

Choosing your flowers

You have probably given some thought to the colour theme of your garden long before you started the process of creating it for, as the title of this book suggests, you will have seen gardens that you have admired or wish to emulate. There are numerous theories about colour, what goes with what; which colours should be close to the house and what colours are a definite 'no-no' in polite society. In garden design books, colour wheels and charts abound often accompanied by complicated instructions in how to use them. For every advocate of using soft, pastel colours, there is another demanding the use of fiery reds and strident yellows. This suits many people but not those of us who just long for a simple way to work these issues out – and, of course, there is a simple way.

In nature, colour clashes are moderated by the greenery of stems and leaves so you can be more adventurous in the garden than you would be indoors.

Providing you have the confidence to put colours together who is to say that you are wrong? Much of what is considered 'acceptable' where colour is concerned is to do with fashion which, by the nature of the beast, is constantly changing. Follow your own instincts, be a free thinker and let

Flower combinations – the spikes of
Salvia nemerosa 'Amethyst' contrast in
colour and form with the rounded flowers
of wild red field poppies

Flower combinations – in this striking
contrast of colour a bi-coloured rose is
surrounded by a sea of *Lychnis coronaria*

Flower combinations – white Icelandic
poppies growing through our native
white campion

Colour combinations – although the
shade of yellow is identical, contrast is
created by the very different flower
shapes of *Lysimachia* and *Inula*

others follow you. The joy of gardening is in experimentation and when you get a winning combination of plants you will be spurred on to try other mixes; likewise if it doesn't work, the offending plant can always be replanted somewhere else and another tried in its place.

But perhaps you do want to follow a fashion trend or recreate the colour scheme you have seen elsewhere. There is nothing wrong with that either for, with gardening, you can change the plants (and your mind) as often as you wish and budget allows. You may decide that, every few years, you want to create a completely different look to the garden which involves the total removal of all that is there. This would be a pity for much pleasure can be obtained from watching a garden develop and mature over the years.

A touch of magenta enhances the colours in this blue border and is echoed by the fading flowers of the salvia

The more you restrict your colour choice – especially if you also limit the type of plants you want to grow – the harder it becomes to find a good range that will flower over many months. This can be overcome with the clever use of foliage so that the blooms have a good background to display against or by planting them in tight groups interspersed with greenery. Some plants have been bred in a broad spectrum of colours – roses or dahlias, for example – but most come with just a choice of few. Remember too when planting a single colour themed border, that other colours need not be totally excluded, for the careful inclusion of a small number of another hue emphasises the dominance of the main colour. Don't introduce too many extra colours; it is best to stick with just one or two.

The rules that apply to texture in leaves also apply to flowers so mix up the shapes by putting spiky flowers with loose, floppy ones or daisy shapes. It is all very much easier to do in practice than it sounds and if you are unfamiliar with the many plants that are available take a trip to your local garden centre and have a look at what is on offer. Quite often they have plant displays where the principles of colour and texture have been put into practice for you.

Try out your own ideas by grouping plants together to see what they look like and whether you like them – in the garden centre trolley if need be.

Pots and planters

The careful positioning of planters can make a dramatic change to the appearance of your garden. Don't just put them in the obvious places such as the edge of patios but also place them where they will draw the eye to create vistas or interest in an otherwise dull corner.

Whatever type you choose – contemporary or traditional – it is important that the plants in them are well maintained. This is much easier to achieve the larger the pot is and it is usually best to avoid having too many small pots dotted at random which can make a garden look very untidy. Watering is required much less frequently with larger pots which is an important consideration if you are short of time.

Hedges – which ones to choose

Most hedges create structural and textural interest in the garden by their height and shape, but they can also be a good source of colour and not just with their leaves. Some hedges are grown specifically for their flowering, although because of pruning restrictions these are usually less formal.

Table 1: Choice of hedge

Name	Colour	Flower or leaf?	Month	Formal or informal?
Beech	Dark red or green	Leaf (turns golden and lasts through winter)	Spring to autumn	Formal
Hornbeam	Green	Leaf	Spring to autumn	Formal
Hawthorn	White	Flower	Spring	Informal
Rose	All except blue	Flower	Summer to autumn	Informal
Lavender	Purple	Flower	Summer	Informal
Osmanthus	White	Flower Evergreen leaf	Spring	Formal or informal
Holly	Green or variegated	Leaf	Evergreen	Formal
Conifers	Green	Leaf	Evergreen	Formal
Yew	Green	Leaf	Evergreen	Formal
Box	Green	Leaf	Evergreen	Formal
Laurel	Green	Leaf	Evergreen	Formal
Prunus cerasifera 'Pisardii'	Pink	Flowers Red leaf	Spring	Formal

Opposite: This carefully placed urn draws the eye, giving added height and interest throughout the year

CHAPTER THREE

Getting the Planting Right

The different types of plants

When we use the term 'plants' we are being very unspecific and there are a number of different words that are used to categorise the different sorts of plants. Although it isn't essential to know these, it does help if the most frequently encountered are recognised for they instantly tell you something about their growth.

Bulbs, corms and tubers

Although botanically bulbs, corms and tubers are different, they are grouped together as they all carry out the same function: they store food for the plant which dies back after flowering to below ground level before re-growth starts once again. Tulips and daffodils are flowers that grow from bulbs.

Annuals

Annuals are plants that flower in their first year of growth and then die. Some types are sold as 'bedding plants'. You can buy seeds or seedlings of many different sorts and grow them on yourself.

Bi-annuals

There are a few varieties of garden plants which flower in their second year of growth and then die.

Perennials (or herbaceous perennials)

These are plants that die back to ground level for the winter months, re-grow each spring and live for a number of years. Ornamental grasses and ferns can be included here for simplicity.

Shrubs

Varying greatly in size, shrubs can live for many years developing a branched, woody framework from ground level. They form much of the structure of the garden, many flowering and/or having interesting leaves or bark. They can be evergreen (keep their leaves throughout the winter) or deciduous (lose their leaves for the winter).

Trees

Whether evergreen or deciduous there is a suitable sized tree for every garden. Some can be very long lived, grow to enormous size and cast shade, so place them carefully.

The heavily scented flowers of lilac, a shrub that loses its leaves in winter

Deciding upon your plant mix

Mixing the different types of plants is a matter of individual taste so you are free to do whatever you like to create the look that you want. You can combine all of the above categories in one large border if you wish, but it is necessary to remember the ultimate size that the plants will grow to and leave adequate space for their development – this is especially true of trees and shrubs although many of these can be pruned to keep them within bounds.

Herbaceous borders

These are the backbone of many a garden open to the public for it is possible to have a display of blooms from spring through to the first frosts of autumn. They can be quite labour demanding, although there are ways to make them much less so (see page 120), and they certainly do have the 'wow' factor that we are striving for.

Cottage garden borders

This style of gardening evolved from the necessity of providing our own food coupled with our natural love of flowers. In its pure form it is a mix of vegetables, herbs, fruit and flowers, however these days mostly it is a style of flower border, usually a more chaotic version of the herbaceous border.

A densely planted border leaves little room for weeds to grow

Shrub borders

These are a combination of shrubs using colour and texture of leaves as their main interest – although many do flower over long periods as well. Weed control can be an issue, although the use of bark mulch (page 105) or ground-cover plants can solve many of these problems. Allowing the lawn to grow up to the edge of the shrubs can also be an option and creates a less formal look.

Mixed borders

These are, as might be expected, a combination of all categories of plants. By combining the different types, it is possible – and often easier – to create a border with all-year appeal. Bulbs flower from January right through to the autumn, with shrubs and herbaceous plants adding to the display until the bark, stems and structure of shrubs, some evergreen, take us through the winter months.

The red and silver branches of an Acer stand out well against a backdrop of tall evergreens

A bold planting of daisies brighten up a border. The flat heads of *Achillea* 'Terracotta' add both contrast and texture and also bring out the honey colours in the old stone wall

How you plant for maximum effect

The simplest way to achieve visual impact is to plant enough of the same plant. If you are considering trees or shrubs that grow to a large size one may be all that is needed. For shrubs, herbaceous plants, grasses and ferns that are more modest in size, plant in groups of three or more of the same variety. Buying large numbers of the same plant can be rather costly. Page 51 shows you how you can do this without breaking the bank.

Odd numbers work better visually than even: if the space dictates that you need more than one, then plant in threes, fives or even sevens.

Using plants repetitively

Another way to achieve drama and cohesion in the garden is to plant the same variety at regular intervals in the border. It is also a useful method to link visually different parts of the garden, although if you do this throughout the whole garden it can become boring. Remember

A zany but effective example of repetitive planting

too, that some plants disappear in the winter: if you need all-year effect consider using evergreen shrubs or a plant that retains good structure.

Nice plant, wrong place

The most common mistake that all of us make is giving in to the temptation to buy a plant on impulse. We take it home and then wonder where to plant it – it usually gets put in the only (and usually totally wrong) vacant space we have at the time or, worse still, allowed to die still in its pot forgotten. This is not only sad it's also demoralising and an expensive waste of money. Those that do get planted and thrive look lonely and out of place and give the border a 'bitty' look. The strange thing about this scenario is that we don't often learn from our mistake – we do it over and over again.

Plants that have outgrown their space do not always have to be removed for, quite often, they can be reduced in size, either by pruning if they are trees or shrubs or by 'splitting' if they are herbaceous plants. The techniques for doing this are the same as for potted plants described on page 52. It will be necessary to dig up the plant first and then replant.

There are a number of plants – relatively few – that require specific soil conditions to thrive. Rhododendrons, as the example mentioned earlier, will not tolerate lime resulting in a plant that gradually sickens with yellowing leaves before dying. If your soil is not suitable you will need to spend much time and effort nurturing these plants if they are to look good, time that can be better spent elsewhere.

When to plant

Pot-grown plants can be planted at any time of year although autumn and spring are best as the ground is usually moist and warm; avoid planting during extreme heat or frost.

During the winter months, bare-rooted and rootballed trees and hedges are also available. These should be planted as soon as possible to prevent their roots from drying out, even if this is just a temporary position. Rootballed plants usually have their root system and soil wrapped in wire mesh and hessian, sometimes with an outer plastic covering. The latter should be removed prior to planting, but leave the mesh and hessian in place as they will quickly biodegrade once buried.

Where to buy your plants

There are a number of places where plants can be bought, all with their advantages and disadvantages.

Where to buy your plants

Source	Advantages	Disadvantages
Garden centres/DIY stores	Plants clearly priced and come with descriptive labels Plants often in flower when offered for sale	Choice often restricted to the most commercial varieties
Specialist nurseries	Very enthusiastic and knowledgeable, a good source of information Often available in smaller pot sizes and in quantity	Plant choice often limited to their specialist field
Plant sales Friends' gardens	Cheap – or free	Plants usually offered are those that spread rapidly which may become a maintenance issue Can be the source of invasive weeds or disease
Mail order	Easy to order, especially if online Unlimited number of sources	Cannot see the actual plants that you are buying Plants can be supplied in disappointingly small sizes – check details closely Sometimes can be more costly
Growing your own	Very inexpensive way of obtaining a large quantity of plants Absorbing and fascinating hobby once you've 'got the bug'	Time consuming Slow method – some plants may take several years to develop fully

How to buy a healthy plant

Unless you are buying plants by mail order (when you have to hope that the quality will be good), it is worth looking at the plants carefully before purchasing.

First of all, take a look at the place that you are buying them from: do you get the impression that they worry about its overall appearance? This doesn't mean that it has to have modern displays and hi-tech gizmos everywhere, but it can tell you a lot about attitudes. Sometimes, especially with smaller specialist nurseries, it can just mean that they are so enthusiastic about the plants that they don't notice anything else. However, if there are lots of plants that have fallen over and look as if they've been lying around for a number of days then tread carefully – in all senses of the meaning.

Next, the plants should look healthy. If they are drooping for lack of water or general TLC it may mean that they aren't being cared for adequately. If the surface of the compost is covered in weeds the plant may have been in stock for quite some time – turn the pot upside down and see if there are roots sticking out the bottom. A few finer ones are quite acceptable but don't purchase it if the roots are thick for it is probable that they will be twisted inside the pot, which doesn't bode well for the plant's future.

Sometimes you will see plants for sale at a reduced price. These can be bargains but make certain that you aren't wasting your money by checking the criteria above.

Plants are often reduced in price when they have stopped flowering or space is required for new season's stock.

It can sometimes be more economical to buy larger sized pots of herbaceous plants if there are numerous shoots emerging from the compost and splitting them into sections with a spade or a knife.

How to plant

To keep your plants in the best condition they should be planted as soon as possible, for if you are too busy to do this you are likely to be too busy to keep them well watered while they are still in their pots. They can dry out very quickly and if this happens the compost usually won't rehydrate by just pouring water onto the surface. To rehydrate your plants you need to plunge the pots into a bucket of water, deep enough to cover the surface. The time often recommended is 30 minutes (which may be the case for very large pots that won't fit in buckets anyway), but if you have a number of plants this will take far too long. Plunging them until air bubbles have stopped rising to the surface is usually adequate and if you come across the odd one that still looks a bit dry you can always do it again. It is worthwhile to plunge before planting regardless of the compost's moisture level unless it is already very wet, for the plants seem to establish quicker and need less watering afterwards.

Place your plants, still in their pots, in the places that you think they should go then stand back and check that they look right and will create the effect that you want to achieve. They may look small and lonely now but remember that you should account for their eventual size. With slower growing plants you can always fill the temporary gaps with shorter lived herbaceous or annuals.

All plants, regardless of their type, should have a hole dug that is wide enough for you to easily backfill with soil or compost once the plant is in

This plant has died because it has literally strangled itself with its own roots

position. The bottom of the hole also needs to be loosened with a fork so that their roots can readily penetrate but it shouldn't be made so deep that the top of the plant's compost is lower than the surrounding soil level. Although adding composts and fertilisers to the planting hole is sometimes recommended this often isn't necessary and it can prevent roots spreading out to search for food.

Remove the plant from its pot and if the roots are congested or spiralling around the compost, tease some of them loose; in severe cases you may need to use a knife or secateurs to cut through them. This may sound drastic but once they start growing tightly around themselves they may continue to do this, literally strangling themselves with their own roots.

Place the plant in the hole and as you backfill firm the loose soil to get rid of air pockets and to prevent the plant rocking within it. Do this with your fingertips rather than your palms or, with larger plants, the heel of your foot, for the aim is to firm but not compact the soil. Finally, water in well – this watering also helps to settle the soil and eradicate air pockets within it.

Staking trees

If you have planted a tree it is a good idea to support it with a stake while it is establishing a strong root system to prevent wind rock. If the tree has a relatively small root ball or was purchased bare rooted a single stake is adequate in all but the windiest sites. In these situations, or if it has a wider root ball, a double stake joined by a crossbar is necessary. In all cases avoid hitting the roots and leave enough space for the trunk to thicken as it grows. A number of different fixings are available ranging from rubber blocks to webbing – avoid wire that will cut into the growing bark.

The stakes should be removed as soon as the tree has established itself, which usually takes a couple of years.

Remember to loosen any ties periodically to prevent damage to the tree as it grows.

When to water your plants

Without water plants die but watering after they have become established in open ground is only rarely required. In dry conditions and with free draining pots it is important to watch for the first signs of plant stress, usually leaves and flowers drooping, and to water as soon as – or ideally before – this is noticed. Different plants have different tolerances depending on the variety and also their situation so it isn't usually necessary to water everything just because one plant looks poorly.

Watering should, ideally, be carried out in the evening as evaporation will be less but there is little evidence that watering when the sun is shining is harmful, as is often cited. It is important, however, that you give your plants a good soaking rather than a lot of small waterings which will only bring their roots to the surface making them more susceptible to drought.

There are many different types of hosepipes, sprinklers and watering systems on the market and often selection just comes down to personal choice. Fully automated systems can be useful, especially if you like gadgets, but they are expensive to install and some plants will often be watered unnecessarily. They do have the advantage of being discreet and saving you time taking out and putting away lengths of hosepipe – something you should always do if you want your garden to look its best.

CHAPTER FOUR

'Must Have' Plants

Useful plants for your garden

There are certain plants you should consider using for a number of reasons. Some of these are commonly found in gardens but should not be dismissed for that reason alone; some are less frequently encountered and worth seeking out. The plants named here are included because I like and use them frequently – this is only your starting point for, over time, you will create your own list which may well change over the years as your taste changes.

Your own list of 'must have' plants for your garden should always reflect your own taste and style or you will never be satisfied with it.

In the following list – which isn't exhaustive – you will see that both the common English plant names (where there is one) and the Latin names are used. The reason for including the Latin is because it is the universal name whereas the common name can differ even from region to region of the same country. You don't need to include every item on this list in your garden!

Trees

If you only have room for one or two trees in your garden, consider planting a fruit tree. Apples, pears and plums have a lot going for them: they are smothered in blossom in spring, give you edible fruit in the autumn and grow to a range of different heights dependent on what root stock they have.

- *Amelanchier* – can be bought as a tree or a shrub. Makes a good ornamental cherry substitute having white blossom in spring and good autumn colour. Unlike cherries, which are disease prone, amelanchiers appear to be unaffected by anything.

- **Birch** – *Betula* **species (spp)** – for medium to larger gardens. Don't give much shade and mostly are grown for their coloured (usually white or silvery) bark. Great against a backdrop of evergreens in winter. There is a small, weeping variety which can look squat and heavy.

- **Handkerchief tree** – *Davidia involucrata* – can take 20 years before it flowers (technically they're not flowers at all) which when it does look like scented, white pocket handkerchiefs hanging from its branches. The tree is quite fast growing and can grow quite large so is only really suitable for larger gardens.

- **Crab apples** – *Malus* **(spp)** – a small tree that is suitable for any size garden. Smothered in blossom in spring followed by miniature sized apples that are very ornamental in the autumn. They are inedible unless you can turn them into crab apple jelly in the kitchen.

- **Mulberry** – *Morus nigra* – only grow this tree if you have enough space to accommodate its low, spreading branches, although they can be grown as a labour-intensive avenue of tightly clipped 'mop heads' on long, clean trunks. It is very late to come into leaf and drops its squishy red, edible fruits everywhere. Later it has good, yellow autumn leaf colour. According to Gerard writing in the 16th century, when it finally does come into leaf spring frosts have ended. An old wives' tale? I rely upon this totally for planting out tender, summer plants and the mulberry has never let me down once.

- **Purple leaf plum** – *Prunus cerasifera* 'Pissardii' – a fast-growing ornamental tree grown for its leaf colour. Has pink flowers in spring and occasionally small fruits. Very twiggy and can be pruned so good for screening, even though it loses its leaves in winter. You can even cut it down and make a hedge of it. Suitable for any size garden.

- **Rowan** – *Sorbus* **species (spp)** – a smaller tree that will fit most gardens. Does not give too much shade and has good flowers, pink, white or orange berries and autumn leaf colour making it great value for the space it occupies. Avoid the larger species of *Sorbus* known as Whitebeam unless you have space for it to flourish.

Most trees and shrubs respond to pruning and shaping, especially in their early years, but you can leave them alone if you prefer.

Shrubs

- *Abelia floribunda* – in hard winters this evergreen, wide spreading shrub can lose its leaves but they soon regrow again in the spring, in some varieties with a lovely coppery tone to them. Palest pink, trumpet flowers smother the plant from summer onwards.

- **Box** – *Buxus sempervirens* – despite the constant threat of box blight, a new disease for which there is no cure, box is useful in so many ways. Its classic use is in topiary: clip it into whatever shape you like – peacocks, racing cars; I prefer low hedges or simple balls or pyramids that can be used to give a degree of formality and structure to a garden. Left unpruned it will very slowly reach a great height but take many years to achieve it. Box grows in full sun or deep shade.

This tiny box parterre is kept beautifully maintained

- **Mexican orange blossom** – *Choisya ternata* – a useful, evergreen shrub that can be pruned to keep it within bounds and even clipped to make an informal hedge. The variety called Aztec Pearl is less vigorous than the type and also more delicate looking. The harsh colour of the yellow-leafed variety, Sundance, makes it difficult to place well in the garden but all have sweetly scented clusters of white flowers throughout spring and summer.

- **Smoke bush** – *Cotinus cogyggria* – a deciduous shrub that can grow quite tall but again responds to pruning. Grown mostly for its ornamental foliage, the purple-leafed varieties increase both in the colour and size of its leaf when pruned. Try planting them in herbaceous borders and cutting them to 15cm above ground level to get long wands of enormous leaves with intense colour.

- *Euonymus fortunei* – you may be surprised to find something as common – and often despised because of that – in this list. As ground cover for difficult places it is extremely useful, its evergreen foliage brightening up shady spots. Give it a wall and it will slowly cling to it, climbing high

The purple-leafed smoke bush, *Cotinus cogyggria* 'Royal Purple'

without the issues associated with ivy, or use it as clipped, low edges to borders. It is also useful for planting at the feet of evergreens or gawky stemmed shrubs, visually anchoring them to the ground. Emerald Gaiety is the silver-edged variety, Emerald 'n' Gold, the brighter yellow variegated leafed one which will become less vivid in colour the deeper into shade it goes – useful if you don't like it too bright.

- *Forsythia* a foolproof, tough shrub, its bare branches smothered in yellow flowers is a mainstay of spring gardens. In a small garden they can be almost too strident in colour and when not in flower they must be one of the most boring plants out. Usually neglected, they look their best when they are pruned hard after flowering. An even better but rarely seen method of growing is to train them against a north wall.

Forsythia grown as a wall-trained shrub

- **Fuchsia** – *Fuchsia megallanica* – we're not talking here of the gaudy, oversized flowers so popular for tubs and hanging baskets. *Fuchsia megallanica* is the small-flowered variety that makes huge towering hedges in coastal gardens. Inland, they are much more modest in size and, in the spring, can be chopped down to whatever height you want. Apart from the standard red and purple flowered combination there is a delicate 'white' version (in reality the palest of pinks). *Fuchsia megallanica* 'Alba'.

- *Hydrangea* – if you're not very keen on the 'mop head' varieties that are often seen by front doors covered in bright pink flowers you may prefer *Hydrangea arborescens* 'Annabelle' which produces large flowerheads of creamy white. Easy to grow and best in light shade – it usually looks very poor and straggly when offered for sale but soon grows strongly once planted. *Hydrangea petiolaris* is the climbing hydrangea that is so useful for covering shady walls but don't underestimate its potential size.

- **Lavender** – *Lavendula* – hardly needs a description for nearly everyone is familiar with the scented, purple flower spikes and silvery foliage that makes up this low-growing shrub. Sadly, they are often seen in gardens growing gaunt and straggly, full of bare wood. This is usually due to lack of pruning and over-rich soil, both of which are discussed on page 161. They are wonderful shrubs for lining paths – let them fall over the edge so that you brush against them as you pass to release their wonderful perfume. Lavenders don't just come in purple: there are pink and white flowered varieties too. The hardiest lavenders are the English and Dutch varieties, the French lavenders that have become widely available in recent years are not nearly as tough.

Lavender grown as a low hedge lining a path

- *Osmanthus x burkwoodii* – this evergreen shrub is faster growing than most books claim. It can reach 3m in height and also can be quite broad but it clips well and so is useful to make into large, topiary-like balls. Whether you let it do its own thing or decide to hard clip, its small leaves will be covered with scented white flowers in spring.

- **Russian sage** – *Perovskia* – rarely growing higher than 1m, its silvery branches and leaves that become smothered by tiny mauve-blue flower spikes during the summer are invaluable in a sunny shrub or herbaceous border; it looks stunning when planted in large groups. To keep it growing strongly and looking good prune it hard (page 163).

- **Mock orange** – *Philadelphus* (spp) – there is a mock orange for every garden for they come in a number of sizes from quite small to huge. The one thing they all do have in common is their white flowers in midsummer that fill the air with scent. They respond to being pruned hard after flowering but this needn't be done every year if you can't be bothered. *Philadelphus microphyllus* is the smallest of them all and useful in repetitive plantings. Everything about it is diminutive apart from its scent; its attractive chestnut-coloured stems are a bonus.

- **Rosemary** – *Rosmarinus* – it may seem odd to find a herb plant here but it is such a showy shrub that it can be planted in borders as well as in a separate herb garden. The widely grown variety is a sprawling shrub that can grow to about 1.2m tall, with a profusion of blue flowers in the spring and it continues to flower sporadically until late autumn. Upright growing 'Miss Jessop' has finer, needle-like leaves, a deeper blue flower and grows to 1.8m in height, although both types can be pruned to restrict their size. A low, prostrate variety is sometimes offered and is very attractive but only grows well in very sheltered or seaside gardens. If you are a keen barbecuer grow it close by so that you can tear off branches to throw on the coals as you cook to release its pungent fragrance.

- **Roses** – *Rosa* – there are so many roses that look and smell lovely when they are in flower but for the rest of the year their gaunt, leggy branches with often diseased leaves are unattractive. *Rosa glauca* is one of the exceptions – it is grown mostly for its dusky pink stems and glaucous foliage. Unpruned it becomes tall and loses its colour: prune hard in late winter for a new supply of young, colourful shoots (page 167). *Rosa chinensis* 'Mutablis' is another shrub rose that can be pruned to keep it smaller. It sends out a continuous show of unscented flowers, cerise in bud, opening to pink and fading to apricot, giving it the appearance of a floral sunset. Plant in groups of three or more for the best effect.

Three colours for the price of one – the cerise buds of *Rosa chinensis* 'Mutabilis' fade through pink to apricot as the flowers mature

- *Viburnum* – a very useful and lovely family of shrub, try *Viburnum x bodnantense*: an upright, tall shrub that carries sweetly scented white or pink flowers on bare wood from November to March. Plant it near a path or doorway that you will use regularly during that time of year to get the maximum enjoyment from it.

If a winter flowering shrub looks dull during the warmer months, plant a large-flowered clematis beside it to scramble through and add colour and interest.

- *Viburnum x burkwoodii* is almost evergreen, losing some of its leaves and retaining others over the winter; those that do fall turn orange and red. It is a spring-flowering shrub that can be trained over an archway or against a wall. It will take time for its stiff growing branches to reach the top and requires pruning once it has flowered but the scent makes it all worthwhile.

- *Viburnum x carlcephalum* is similar to *burkwoodii* but loses all its leaves in winter. It flowers in spring and the scent is strong and heady – if you only grow one sort go for this. It looks good as a stand-alone specimen but is equally successful in borders. No *viburnum* likes having its roots disturbed too much so be careful when forking or planting beneath them.

Climbers

Climbers are indispensable in the garden but too often they become unruly and messy. Pruning and how to support them is discussed later but those that follow in this list will not take up too much of your time in sorting out.

- *Clematis* – if you grow the large-flowered varieties they are very straightforward to maintain. They come in shades of white, pink, purple, red, wine and blue and flower from

The large-flowered clematis are very simple to keep looking at their best midsummer onwards. The sorts that are smothered in flowers in spring — the *montanas* — look terrific but do need more care than they usually ever get if they are to look their best. They can be left to do their own thing and totally ignored if you grow them through tall trees where they will look stunning.

- *Hydrangea* — see shrubs.

- **Honeysuckle** — *Lonicera periclymenum* — not all honeysuckles are scented and they are also prone to mildews in late summer, but despite that they are worth a place here. Grow them away from walls where air can circulate freely around them, such as on trees or archways, and clip them immediately after flowering if they get in your way. Grow 'Belgica' for early summer flowers and 'Serotina' for later flowers — both are heavily scented.

Climbers are a great way to get some height in a new garden quickly.

- **Roses** — always a favourite but not always well grown. You will need to feed and dead-head them if you want the more colourful and bred varieties to flower continuously. For ease, assuming you have space for some can grow to 9m or more, try the species climbers such as 'Paul's Himalayan Musk', 'Kiftsgate' or 'Wedding Day' for myriads of tiny pink or white, perfumed flowers. 'Snow Goose' is shorter only reaching about 3m. They will only flower once during the summer but carry hundreds of small, scarlet hips giving autumn interest until the birds eat them.

A white rose has been left to scramble over a large shrub, its flowers mimicking the tiny ones of *Photinia davidiana* 'Palette'

Rosehips in the snow

- **Evergreen jasmine** – *Trachelospermum jasminoides* – with glossy, evergreen leaves and white, jasmine-like, fragrant flowers in summer is far more tolerant of conditions than is often thought. For best results grow it against a south or west-facing wall, especially in colder areas, or grow it on a shady wall of a conservatory. The true jasmines always seem to end up a tangled mass of living and half dead branches so, if you are limited for time, grow this one.

- *Tropaeolum speciosum* – if you like a challenge then this is the plant for you. It may take a number of attempts before you succeed in getting this bright scarlet flowered nasturtium to grow but, when you achieve it, the result is spectacular. Hundreds of tiny flowers all summer long brighten up shady, cool places so long as the roots are not too dry. Try planting it on the north side of clipped evergreen shrubs to show it off at its best. It requires no maintenance whatsoever and will slowly increase in quantity over the years. It doesn't like too much lime in the soil.

- **Vine** – *Vitis* (spp) – if you grow them for grapes you will probably be disappointed but grown for their leaves they are very useful. They need support but will produce welcome shade over a summer pergola, will grow on north-facing walls and the leaf size and colour can vary enormously depending upon your choice. Try *Vitis* 'Brandt' for huge, green ones and *Vitis vinifera* 'Purpurea' for smaller, ruby coloured. Although they can be controlled in size it is best to grow them in fairly large spaces to really see them at their best.

- **Wisteria** – you should only grow wisteria if you have plenty of space and the time to prune their long whippy branches that they send out all summer long. When cared for well (and this isn't complicated) they look wonderful when in full bloom in May.

Herbaceous perennials

There are so many good varieties to choose from that you will find it difficult to know which ones to leave off your list. The majority of the plants here usually require no staking and those that have a tendency to look shabby can be immediately and drastically tidied.

Many herbaceous plants can be cut down at various stages of their lives to keep them looking good. This requires little time and even less skill so your garden continues to look at its best for much longer than normal.

- *Achillea* – chunky, flat flowerheads and strong stems are softened by feathery, grey or sage green foliage. The yellow varieties are good for vibrancy but they also come in shades varying from whites through pinks to brick reds and orange. They may require some support and dead heading but cope without either if you should forget.

- *Agapanthus* – it is often said that these only flower well when grown in pots with their root congested. In well drained, sunny borders they can do even better. Native to South Africa, some varieties are hardier than others so check the labels carefully when buying.

- **Ladies Mantle** – *Alchemilla mollis* – its fresh young leaves hold water droplets that sparkle in the morning sunlight. Frothy green-yellow flower spikes are produced in profusion and it will self-seed if allowed to. As soon as it starts to look shabby cut off every leaf and flower to ground level and new ones will appear within days. Use it to edge borders and pathways, under shrubs and in difficult, shady places – it will grow anywhere. There is a much smaller version that needs no maintenance whatsoever, *Alchemilla conjuncta*, with very pretty, darker green leaves edged with silvery hairs.

- **Japanese anemone** – *Anemone hupehensis, Anemone x hybrida* – first a word of warning: Japanese anemones are difficult to eradicate once you have planted them as every piece of broken root will regrow. They will run riot in the flower border – albeit prettily with their tall pink or white flowers each autumn. Put yours in dry, shady places or amongst shrubs where they can do no harm. The white flowers will brighten up a dark corner. You will find there are many different varieties with English names growing to varying heights.

- **Michaelmas daisy** – *Aster* – some Michaelmas daisies are prone to mildew which spoils their appearance just as they are about to bloom. One that you shouldn't have any trouble with is the variety called 'Monch', with sprays of lavender blue flowers from late July onwards. They may require some support unless you give them the haircut treatment known as the 'Chelsea chop' – see page 177 for details.

- **Giant forget-me-not** – *Brunnera macrophylla* – these coarse-leaved plants send out their vivid blue flowers in spring and are really useful for giving early interest. Treat them in the same way as *Alchemilla* (see above) or the leaves become very shabby. There are some variegated varieties with cream markings which are pretty but can become sun scorched, so plant these in shadier spots.

- **Bellflower** – *Campanula* – there are many varieties of bellflower and often the ones that are being sold cheaply at village fetes spread too vigorously to be included in a list of useful plants – you will spend too many hours trying to keep them under control. The two that you should consider are *Campanula persicifolia*, a dainty variety that self-seeds happily but is never troublesome, and *Campanula lactiflora*, taller and clump forming with densely packed flower heads. Both come in whites and blues and with *lactiflora* look out for 'Pritchard's Variety' (purple) and 'Loddon

Anna' (pinkish) – try mixing the latter with a white-flowered version for an interesting combination.

- **Valerian – *Centranthus rubra*** – a tough, mid-height plant with glossy green leaves and pink or white flowers. Try to buy in flower as some of the pinks can be 'dirty' – make sure you get the deeper coloured ones. Useful for dry, sunny corners and at the foot of sound walls for valerian's roots can dislodge loose stone or brickwork. If you are lucky it will be visited by the fascinating hummingbird hawk moth, an uncommon summer visitor that, as its name implies, takes nectar from the flowers hovering on the wing like a tiny version of its namesake.

- **Plume thistle – *Cirsium rivulare* 'Atropurpureum'** – tall, strong stems growing from a basal rosette of leaves, their burgundy coloured flowerheads act as magnets for bumblebees. They grow best in full sun although they can cope with some shade – if they get too dry they tend

The plume thistle, Cirsium rivulare 'Atropurpureum'

Monkshood is a good alternative option to delphinium

to suffer from mildew. If this happens, cut off the foliage and water the plant well or, as the leaves can look rather coarse as the season progresses, plant something else in front to disguise both them and the mildew. They flower from midsummer into late autumn. Leave the seedheads in place to be visited by feeding goldfinches.

- *Delphinium* – when grown in large groups, delphiniums look spectacular. However, looking good does involve some effort – slugs love to eat their new shoots and they will probably require staking to keep them upright. If that is all too much bother, you can always use monkshood (*Aconitum*) as an alternative. They are coarser (and poisonous so a little caution is required when handling them) but their 1.5m blue, purple or white flowering stems never need staking.

Although it is possible to buy plants that have been bred on short stems to avoid staking, often they can look rather out of proportion.

Many foxgloves have randomly spotted 'throats'

- **Foxglove** – *Digitalis purpurea* – the loveliest foxgloves are those that grow wild in this country. They make good garden plants when planted in groups of no less than five with their tall spikes of white, apricot or pink flowers much visited by bumblebees. Although the plants often die in their second year they will have self-sown and the resulting seedlings can be left to grow where they are or moved somewhere else. The white take on a luminous quality when grown in damp, shady corners or amongst shrubs and trees.

- **Blue lyme grass** – *Elymus arenarius* – a silvery leafed grass that looks spectacular when grown in large pots. To keep them looking neat, cut off all the leaves in early spring and just remember to water it occasionally. In the autumn the leaves often turn straw coloured and can be left throughout the winter. Don't be tempted to plant in the border as its running root system will prove troublesome to control.

Oposite: Blue lyme grass looks spectacular when grown in a large pot

- *Geranium* – we are not talking about the bright red summer bedding plants so beloved by our grandmothers (which are really *Pelargoniums*). The true geraniums are tough, hardy plants that come in so many different varieties and heights that it is often difficult to decide which ones to choose for there are few that you will be disappointed with. *Geranium* 'Tanya Rendall' is a low-growing plant with small pink flowers that can bloom from May through to Christmas. Plant it somewhere you will appreciate its unusual chocolate-brown leaves. *Geranium* 'Sanne' is similar, slightly taller and not quite so long flowering if you prefer a white version. *Geranium pratense* is a British native plant that flowers midsummer, in white, mauve or blue. There are a number of varieties including double flowered ones – an especially lovely one is 'Mrs Kendall Clark', a single with pale blue-mauve flowers, the petals faintly streaked with darker markings. A good planting combination is *Geranium pratense* grown amongst shrub roses where its 60cm flower spikes can scramble and climb amongst them. Equally at home growing in the border or alongside shrubs or other shady spots, *Geranium phaeum* is an upright, taller plant. Commonly known as 'Mourning Widow' because of its small, dark maroon flowers, there is a white-flowered version which is very lovely and shows up well. If geraniums start to look shabby, which they can do once

Geranium pratense 'Mrs Kendall Clark'

they have had their first flush of flowers, cut them as you would *Alchemilla* (see above) and new leaves and flowers will quickly reappear (not the *macrorhizuum* or *renardii* types).

Remember that most herbaceous plants look better when they are planted in groups of the same type so do buy enough of them. The majority will give you many years of pleasure so the initial investment is well worthwhile.

- **Hellebore, Lenten rose** – *Helleborus orientalis* – plant these close to the house where you will see their nodding, white through to maroon flowers, some very prettily marked, from late winter through to May. If you remember, cut off every leaf to ground level when you first start to see the flower buds pushing through the ground for these often become shabby and hide the flowers just as they come into bloom. This procedure also controls a blotch disease that leaves unsightly black marks and streaks on the foliage.

- **Day lily** – *Hemerocallis* – although the flowers only last for 24 hours they are sent up in such profusion that they give colour for months on end. They are robust enough to be planted amongst shrubs providing they have enough sun. In the border they are especially useful as they send up their new, strap-like leaves early in the year although they do not begin to flower until June.

- *Iris* – the large-flowered iris is spectacular but rather a luxury as its period in bloom is so short. Its long, knobbly root system (rhizomes), reminiscent of ginger roots, need to be planted shallowly so that the top of them are showing above ground where they can be sun baked. Plant in the front of the border and do not let other, more vigorous plants shade it. They come in myriad colours and

A contrast of flower shape gives additional interest but the golden colour of the *Achillea* is linked by the centres of this day lily

colour combinations and a few are scented – if you can afford the space, devote a whole area just to them for a spectacular, three-week, rainbow display.

- *Liriope muscari* – a late summer-flowering plant with grass-like leaves, perfect for edging a path or placing at the front of the border. Like the blue lyme grass, cut off all the leaves in early spring and then ignore it. From September onwards it will send up short spikes of grape hyacinth-like flowers in purple or white.

- **Mallows** – there are two that are especially useful in the garden and they are not used nearly often enough. *Malva moschata*, the musk mallow, is another British native although it is so exotic looking that it is hard to imagine it is a wild flower. Its finely divided leaves on a branching stem up to almost 1m high are covered in slightly frilled pink or white flowers. Allow it to self-seed which it will do freely – but never in a troublesome way – for blooms from May through to September. Don't be put off by its English name for it has no unpleasant smell whatsoever. *Althaea officinalis*, the marsh mallow, is indeed the plant that the soft, spongy sweets were originally made from. Rarely seen growing as a border plant, you will find it really useful to give height for it can grow up to 1.8m. The palest pinky-mauve flowers with a darker centre, rather like miniature hollyhocks to which they are related, line the stems, complimented with grey-green felty leaves.

The tall, see-through stems of marsh mallow, *Althaea officinalis*, can be placed quite far forward in a border despite their height

that you will not be able to resist stroking each time you pass them by. Marsh mallows slowly increase to make larger clumps and occasionally will self-sow. You probably will not find them in a garden centre but they should be available from herb plant nurseries; they are well worth the effort to find. Unlike hollyhocks, neither of these two mallows suffer from rust, the disease that so disfigures their giant, cottage garden relatives.

- **Black grass – *Ophiopogon planiscapus* 'Nigrescens'** – although it looks just as its common name sounds, it is not a grass at all but related to the lily. Low growing and trouble free it looks stunning when edging a border, especially when interplanted with *Cyclamen hederifolium*. The *Ophiopogon* sends out tiny-flowering spikes of pink flowers in the autumn at the same time as the cyclamen, a combination that will send you into raptures.

- **Peony – *Paeonia*** – a number of peony species are available from specialist nurseries but the ones that are easiest to find and to grow are the named varieties of *Paeonia lactiflora*. It is really a case of you choosing your favourite, but 'Duchesse de Nemours' (white), 'Karl Rosenfeld' (cerise) or 'Sarah Bernhardt' (pink) are all reliable, flowering in June and July.

- **Poppy – *Papaver*** – there are numerous types of poppies and all are useful plants, although the larger ones can get rather untidy. Some are easily grown annuals: just scatter the seed in spring where you want them to grow. The oriental poppies are the big, perennial ones and come in white, red and varying shades of pink. Cut every bit of them down to ground level immediately the first flowers finish and they will regrow fresh new leaves very quickly.

- *Phlox* – one of the mainstays of the traditional summer border for very many years, phlox also work well in more contemporary plantings. There are many named varieties but 'White Admiral' (white), 'Windsor' (cerise) and 'Hesperis' (violet) are tall, scented and reliable although they may require staking if not given the 'Chelsea chop'. Phlox prefer to be grown in semi shade although they will tolerate full sun providing they don't dry out at the roots.

Remember to leave spaces where you can plant bulbs. The majority will flower in the spring giving lots of colour and interest before the herbaceous plants take over.

• **New Zealand Flax, Phormium** – *Phormium tenax* – young specimens can be used in summer pots on their own or as the centrepiece with other plants where their long, strap-like leaves will give both structure and a degree of grandeur. After a couple of years, they can be planted into the garden border, with some shelter from cold winds where, in some years, they send up tall, bronzed flower spikes, more interesting than attractive.

Phormium can grow to a considerable size in favoured places

Those with green or burgundy-coloured leaves are hardier than the multi-coloured varieties. Don't underestimate their potential size although a cold winter will knock them back severely.

- *Polygonum affine* 'Dimity' – a very useful ground-hugging plant with short pink and red flower spikes from June onwards. Through the winter the leaves turn a coppery colour. It requires no care whatsoever and can be used in difficult places, at the front of borders and in shrubberies.

- *Rudbeckia* – if you are fond of yellow sunflowers then Rudbeckias are for you. In varying heights from 1–2.7m, they need no support and flower from July through to the frosts. The taller ones are robust enough to be planted amongst shrubs providing they receive enough sun and they work well when planted in gravel and contemporary gardens.

- Ice plant – *Sedum spectabile* – all the sedums have one thing in common: fleshy, succulent leaves and flattish heads made up of hundreds of tiny flowers. Use this sedum at the front of sunny borders (although they do cope with a little more shade than is usually realised) where its pink to deep reddish-pink, occasionally white, flowers attract butterflies and bees in late summer. It is a squat, bulky looking plant so is useful in repetitive planting and for using in corners as end stops. Although the ice plant doesn't grow too tall, it has an irritating habit of splitting and toppling over under the weight of the flowers so that, just when it is looking at its best, it suddenly flops to reveal ugly stems. You can avoid this by either placing low supports around it or, better still, by giving it the 'Chelsea chop'.

- *Sidalcea* – another disease-free relative of the hollyhock. They form slowly spreading clumps of white or pink flowers and will even do well in partial shade.

- Oat grass – *Stipa gigantea* – even people that aren't too keen on grasses love these: a clump of low-growing, evergreen leaves that produce 1.8m-tall long wands of oat-like flower heads. Despite its size, it can be planted quite close to the front of the border for it is a 'see-through' plant and breaks up the monotony of regular heights. Use it in repetitive planting

Another tall, see-through plant, *Molinia caerulea* 'Transparent'. Its stems turn straw-coloured in autumn

for impressive results or even in gaps amongst tall shrubs. The variety of purple moor grass, *Molinia caerulea* 'Transparent', is a more diminutive and upright grass that can be used in the same way and both colour golden brown in the autumn.

- **Chinese meadow-rue – *Thalictrum delavayii* 'Hewitt's Double'** – if you want something really unusual that creates a lot of interest when it is in flower, then this is the plant for you. Attractive sprays of leaves, reminiscent of aquilegia or maidenhair fern, sit at ground level giving no hint of the 1.2m-tall flowering stems that break into dozens of tiny purple-mauve hanging buttons. Place it towards the back of a border where it does best in semi-shade and in soil that does not dry out.

- **Foam flower – *Tiarella cordifolia*** – this little evergreen perennial has prettily marked leaves and short tufts of whitish flowers from spring to midsummer. *Tiarella wherryii* is similar but a little later so useful for extending the flowering period into the autumn. Both are excellent for planting in semi shade and at the front of borders.

A number of taller plants such as oat grass and verbena have low-level leaves so it is possible to see between the flowering stalks. These 'see through' plants are useful to give height closer to the front of borders as other shorter plants behind them will still be visible.

- *Verbena bonariensis* – tall, wiry stems break into flattish heads of bright lilac flowers, much visited by bees and butterflies in late summer. Its 'see through' stems mean that it can be planted much further forward than would normally be the case with a plant that can grow to 1.5m tall. It works well in all styles of borders and looks particularly good amongst tall grasses. It likes a sunny spot and may self-sow especially in gravel gardens. If *bonariensis* is too tall for your requirement there is the shorter *Verbena hastata* which is similar but more prone to dying out over the winter.

- *Veronica gentianoides* – a low ground-cover plant with glossy green leaves that send up short spikes of powder blue flowers in spring. The perfect plant for the front of the border which needs very little care.

Bulbs

Spring-flowering bulbs are one of the mainstays of the garden and you will never have too many of them. They are great grown in outdoor pots or brought into the house or to give away in flower as gifts. There are so many to choose from that you will soon be wondering which ones to leave off your list. Not all bulbs bloom in spring and the list here includes some useful varieties for later flowering.

Bulbs are extremely good value for money, with many types lasting for years and increasing in number.

- *Alliums* – don't be concerned that the alliums are sometimes described as ornamental onions for, although they are, they don't smell at all oniony unless you crush their leaves. Surprisingly, some even have sweetly scented flowers. They do have one major drawback, however: just as they come into flower their leaves start to die back and look shabby. This can be avoided by planting them so that the bases of the alliums – where the leaves are – are hidden by the emerging foliage of other plants. Alliums are useful in the garden because they flower after the daffodils and tulips but before the majority of herbaceous plants, giving floral interest at a time when the borders can look a little flat. There are dozens of different varieties to choose from; two to avoid, because they can self-seed so freely that they become a nuisance, are *Allium triquetrum* and *Allium ursinum*, our native wild garlic, that carpets damp woodland floors. All alliums are 'see through' plants and the majority flower in May and June. Here are some of the best:

- *Allium* **'Purple Sensation'** – one of the most popular choices and for good reason, having tall 75cm stems topped with large, round heads of a good, deep mauve. Like most alliums, the flower heads are made up of hundreds of tiny flowers much loved by bees. Plant in groups or weave throughout the border. Also like most alliums this will self-sow but, unlike the examples above, it is easily controlled if you want to.

- *Allium bulgaricum* – also known as *Nectoscordum siculum* – is taller, growing to 1m with hanging green, white, brown and red bells, a strange combination that you will either love or hate. It will create a lot of interest in your garden.

- *Allium cernuum* – small, hanging heads of an intense rose pink make it quite different in appearance to the majority of alliums. Also, unlike other bulbs, when you buy them they often look like a shrivelled bunch of supermarket spring onions but once in the ground they soon revive. Surprisingly, their foliage remains fresher looking than the other alliums during flowering so planting them at the front of the border where their pretty flowers can be most appreciated is not a problem. Plant them in tight groups to show them to their best advantage. They grow to 35cm and flower a little later than most of the other alliums.

- *Allium christophii* – confusingly, some alliums are sold under more than one name so occasionally you may find it named *Allium albopilosum*. It is a shorter plant of 50cm with large, globe flower heads made up of many individual lilac star-like flowers. These have a metallic sheen to them and are good candidates for cutting and drying, or leave them on the plant where they will continue to give interest for many months.

Opposite: Alliums are easy to grow and are useful as many flower when there is a dip in floral interest in the garden

- *Allium cowanii* and *Allium neopolitanum 'Grandiflorum'* – two different alliums, placed here together because they are so similar in appearance. Pure white flowers that are very sweetly scented and great for cutting appear in May. Cowanii is shorter in height at 35cm, whereas Grandiflorum grows to 60cm.

- *Allium schubertii* – for those of us old enough to remember, the shape of these flowers are reminiscent of a sputnik, with an explosion of small deep pink stars at the end of irregular length stalks. They are great plants for children to grow for they love the oddity of their flowers, which really do look like something out of a science fiction comic. They grow to 40cm and are best planted close to a path where their strange flowers (which are also good for drying) will be noticed and create interest and comment, although their foliage does need to be concealed somewhat.

- *Allium sphaerocephalum* – fortunately this allium does have an easier English name, the drumstick allium, which describes the shape of their small maroon flower heads perfectly. Growing to 60cm you can plant them in groups or, better still, scatter them throughout the border and plant them where they fall.

- *Allium tuberosum* – **Garlic chives** – these are easiest found in the herb section of garden centres for their flat, mild-tasting, garlic-flavoured leaves can be used in salads. In the border they are a useful addition with 60cm-tall white flower heads that can flower late into the autumn.

- *Camassia* – spikes of blue or white flowers last for weeks during May and June and look good growing in borders or naturalised in grass. At Highgrove, Prince Charles grew the taller types combined with 'Queen of the Night' tulips to stunning effect, something which you can easily emulate, even in the smallest of gardens. There isn't a bad camassia to try: *Camassia esculenta* is a shorter (and very much cheaper) plant with a deep blue flower, *Camassia cusickii*, 1.2m, and *Camassia leichtlinii*, 85cm, are taller growing and more elegant. All can have leaves that need concealing, although when growing in grass this is neither an option or necessary.

There are bulbs suitable for every aspect and condition and they look especially good when planted in a natural setting and allowed to spread.

- *Crocus* – there are three different types of crocus that are worth trying in your garden, the standard large-flowered variety and the smaller flowering species, both of which flower in spring, and the autumn-flowering species. All are very easy to grow but you may have to take precautions against mice which love to eat the tiny, round corms as you plant them. If you don't fancy trapping the mice you can grow crocus in pots and plant them as they flower or as the flowers fade for you will find that they are rarely troubled at that stage or afterwards. Perhaps the mice like the growing shoot as it emerges from the corm which is often present at the time of planting.

  Spring-flowering crocus come with a lot of variation in a limited colour range of whites, blues, purples and yellows. It takes a large quantity to have real impact in a garden, especially of the smaller varieties. All are worth growing so buy those that you like the look of best and plant them anywhere you like – in borders, pots or the lawn where their fine leaves and early flowering have no impact upon the mowing regime.

  You will rarely come across autumn-flowering crocus in the garden which is a pity. The most easily obtained is *Crocus speciosus*, its violet flowers appearing in September or October. There is a beautiful white version, *Crocus speciosus* 'Albus' which is worth seeking out despite being usually double the price of the standard colour. *Crocus sativus* is the meadow saffron, the source of the food colouring – it is in my experience a little more difficult to grow well than *Crocus speciosus*.

  Often sold as autumn crocus because they resemble them, *Colchicum* is in comparison, robust and chunky. There are both single and double types. Their huge bulbs will flower even when left unplanted – try placing them on a flat dish or in a basket and packing them with moss for use as an impressive, indoor table decoration. Left as they are they will flower without any further attention or water and can be planted in the garden as soon as the blooms fade. Unlike the true autumn crocus, Colchicum send out large strap-like leaves in early spring that must be given room to grow and die down naturally. It is because they flower without leaves that colchicums are sometimes sold named as 'Naked Ladies'.

- *Cyclamen* – here we are talking of the hardy cyclamen not the giant-flowered varieties sold as house plants, although these can look good in outdoor pots for dramatic, if somewhat short-lived glory. Likewise, in the autumn, smaller flowered cyclamen are sold in full flower and these are excellent in early winter pots and even planted in sheltered places in the garden. When buying these, if scent is important to you, sniff each plant as you select it for some have a lovely perfume when others, even of the same colour, have none. The really hardy and trouble-free cyclamen for the garden is usually sold as a dormant corm – a dried disc that can be, unlike most bulbs, difficult to know which is the top and which is bottom. Plant them in shady spots at the foot of trees or the front of borders where they can remain undisturbed over the years. They can be a little temperamental in establishing but usually settle down after a season or two and then flower every spring or autumn, depending on the variety. As their pink or white flowers fade, their seed heads form and the stem twists like a tightly coiled spring before exploding and scattering its seeds to produce an ever increasing number of new plants. You will never have too many of them. *Cyclamen coum* flowers in spring, whereas *Cyclamen hederifolium* flowers in autumn, the latter often having wonderfully marked and marbled leaves.

- **Winter aconite – *Eranthis* –** single, little buttercup yellow flowers hug the ground, each surrounded by a green choirboy's ruff, from Christmas onwards. They are part of the elite group of flowers that, even where someone doesn't care for the colour yellow, are loved and treasured. Grow them anywhere in your garden where they will slowly self-sow and spread. They die down quickly after flowering so the decaying foliage is not an unsightly problem.

- **Fritillary – *Fritillaria* –** a fashionable group of flowers at the moment but not the easiest to get established. *Fritillaria persica* is one of the more straightforward ones to grow, with 1m spikes of dark maroon, almost brown, bell-like flowers, quite sombre and melancholy, yet fascinating nevertheless. *Fritillaria meleagris* is our native snake's head fritillary also known in some country districts as 'chequers', named one assumes, after the intricate markings of the flowers. In the wild it grows in damp meadows prone to flooding but they are happy enough in the garden border although they still look at their best when growing naturally in grass. They come in varying shades of dusky pink or there is a rather good white version usually sold under its Latin name *Fritillaria meleagris* 'Alba'.

The snake's head fritillary is a rare native but grows happily in our gardens

The crown imperials, *Fritillaria imperialis*, were the fashion plants of the 1950s and 60s and have fallen from grace since then. Triffid-like in appearance, with orange or yellow flower heads on 90cm stalks with tufts of broad, drooping and twisted leaves, they can have quite a pungent, foxy odour. Years ago they were planted singly, standing as sentinels in the border but they look their best when planted randomly through open wooded areas. If you have an area like this, even if it is just a small grove of say five white stemmed birches, try them for they are trouble free and just a bit different from the norm.

- *Snowdrop – Galanthus –* these, along with winter aconites, are the heralds of spring, flowering from January even when the ground is snow covered. If you are already a snowdrop buff, a Galanthophile, you will not need to be told about the huge numbers of different types, each varying only very slightly from one another and hard to tell apart to the untrained eye. For the rest of us, all we need to know is that the common snowdrop comes in single or double flowered varieties. Traditionally they are considered best bought 'in the green' which means that they are sold just as they finish flowering with their leaves and flower heads still attached. These are nearly always bought from specialist mail order nurseries and should be planted immediately when you receive them. Plant them under trees, where they look their best, or towards the back of borders, for however pretty they are in flower, you won't want to see their yellowing, dying leaves once they have finished blooming. Over time they will self-seed and increase in number, something that should be encouraged. If you are impatient, every few years you can dig them up and split the clumps before replanting them again over a wider area.

- **Lily** – *Lilium* – another plant that comes in so many different types, heights and colours. The strongly perfumed varieties that are sold as cut flowers in every supermarket and florist are easy enough to grow but are so exotic in appearance that they can be difficult to place in a garden. Try growing them in pots, among taller 'see-through' plants such as *Verbena bonariensis* or oat grass or, better still, in a designated area devoted to cut flowers where you can harvest them without any guilt pangs. The species lilies usually have more trumpets per stem but of a much smaller size and not as perfumed. These often look better in garden borders just because they do look more natural. Lilies can sometimes fall over because of their height or weight of flower and a way to avoid this or staking is, as with gladioli, to plant them deeper than normal, 15cm or even more. Some varieties send out roots from their stems which when planted at this depth gives them additional stability.

  Lilium 'African Queen' has 1.5m-tall stems topped with a cluster of fragrant, drooping bell-shaped flowers. When planted amongst or behind oat grass their apricot coloured blooms blend beautifully with the autumn tinted, straw coloured stems and seed heads of the grass, a memorable combination. *Lilium regale* is a heavily scented lily which when established sends out large numbers of white, slightly streaked with pink, trumpet-shaped flowers in July on 1.2m-tall stems. *Lilium regale* 'Album' is a little shorter than the type if you prefer a pure white version, sometimes flowering a little earlier too.

  The florist's large-flowered and heavily scented lilies are known as orientals. You will probably select by colour but two that are easy and reliable arc 'Casa Blanca' with huge but balanced white flowers with rust-coloured anthers which like the majority of lilies can stain clothing if brushed against. This can be avoided by snipping them off with scissors, which is reputed to make the flowers last a little longer, but they do also lose some of their dramatic appearance. The other is 'Stargazer', a deep cerise flower edged with white. 'Stargazer' is a little shorter than 'Casa Blanca' at 90cm and 1.2m respectively.

The Turk's cap or martagon lilies are simple and very beautiful for wilder borders or amongst shrubs where their 1.2m multi-flowered stems look most at home. Flowering in June through to August, the martagons come in dusky purple, wine or white.

Lilies are great as cut flowers and are very straightforward to grow whether in pots, in the border or in the greenhouse.

- **Grape hyacinth – *Muscari* –** the common blue-flowered *Muscari armeniacum* spreads rapidly to create blue carpets of flowers in April. They can become rather a nuisance in the border and are best confined to places where they are less bother such as the foot of hedges or fences. More and more varieties are coming onto the market, some more worthy of a place in the garden than others. One that has been around for a long time and nowhere near as rapidly increasing, leafy or tall as the type is *Muscari botryoides* 'Album', with white flowers. Another taller and more refined variety is *Muscari* 'Valerie Finnis' with flowers of a soft blue.

- **Daffodil – *Narcissus* –** the most commonly planted bulb and with good reason: they are easy to grow and they welcome in the spring in a way that no other flower can. They are inexpensive, generally trouble free and are great for picking. Always plant daffodils in groups; nothing looks worse than a single row of them when in flower. If you want to plant them at a foot of a wall or fence where the row effect is inevitable do make sure that you grow lots of them, several bulbs deep, to create impact. It is often possible to buy bags of mixed daffodils but you will find that this can create problems with odd flowering times and colours and rarely looks as good as buying individual varieties and mixing them yourself.

Narcissus 'Golden Harvest' is a large yellow daffodil, with a strong 45cm stem, flowering in early March, Narcissus 'St Keverne' is slightly shorter and blooms just a little later. Narcissus 'Carlton' is another large, yellow daffodil which flowers later still, into early April and of similar height. By blending these three varieties together you can extend the flowering period by quite a number of days. If you wish to add white daffodils to the mix, Narcissus 'Ice Follies' starts off with a yellowish trumpet which soon fades to white and flowers at the same time as 'Carlton'. All of these varieties have fairly large, thick leaves that take time to yellow and die so do not plant at the front of borders where this will be visible.

Keep the standard, large-flowered daffodils at the back of borders or where their dying foliage, which hangs around for weeks, can be hidden under the leaves of other emerging plants.

The *cyclamineus* and *triandus* daffodils are more refined and delicate in appearance although they cope with poor weather conditions just as well as their chunkier relatives. They are easier to place in the garden border as their foliage disappears more quickly and are useful in tubs and pots. *Narcissus cyclamineus* 'Jenny' is white with a pale yellow trumpet which,

The pale yellow trumpet of the daffodil 'Ice Follies' soon fades to white

like 'Ice Follies', soon turns to white. 'Jetfire' is a good variety if you like bi-coloured daffs, yellow with an orange trumpet, while 'Tête-à-tête' and 'February Gold' are pure yellow. All grow to about 30cm and flower from late February to April. *Narcissus triandus* 'Hawera' has the most delicate pale yellow flowers flowering in March whereas 'Petrel' is cream in colour and one of the latest flowering narcissi, blooming in May. Both carry two or three flowers per 25cm stem.

Daffodils perhaps look their loveliest when they are planted in a naturalist way in grass or lining long driveways. More details of their planting and care can be found on page 131.

- Squill – *Scilla siberica* – these diminutive little plants flower and seed freely, soon covering a large area with their intense, electric blue, or sometimes white, single bell-like flowers. It is hard to believe that such tiny plants can have so much impact in a garden. After two months of early spring flowering they die off rapidly so their foliage is not a maintenance issue either. Similar, in the sense that it does the same job, is *Puschkinia libanotica*, a pale silvery-blue or white. Others are *Chionodoxa forbesii* and *Chionodoxa luciliae*, Glory of the Snow, which come in a bright but not as intense blue or in pink or white. Both have multiple bell-like flowers on a single stalk and are a little taller than the squill at 15cm, but all seed and naturalise readily.

- *Tritelia* 'Queen Fabiola' – another little-grown bulb that you should make room for in your garden. In fact, it takes up very little room, is cheap to buy which means you can have loads of them and sends up 45cm high stems with flowers of strong violet-blue. They are great as a cut flower and need no maintenance of any kind. They normally flower in May or June but you can get them to flower later by planting in late spring if you are able to store them somewhere cool and dry until then.

- Tulip – *Tulipa* – how do you create a list of tulips when there are so many different varieties and colours to choose from? If you have already decided upon colour schemes for your borders or pots then this does reduce the choice somewhat. The issues with planting tulips are very different from those of daffodils although they are usually purchased at the same time. It is important to remember that tulips are prone to disease and that the quality of the bloom deteriorates, often quite quickly. This can be reduced by judicious dead-heading and picking up every fallen petal but even dedicated gardeners often don't have the time for that. An alternative is to plant them in baskets before planting the whole thing – the slatted plastic ones used for pond plants are ideal for this – and to lift the baskets from the ground once the tulips are over. Ideally, these are then allowed to die off naturally before replanting the next year in fresh soil. For the majority of us that don't have the space or the inclination to do this there is an easier alternative: each year buy some new ones to 'top up' and to remove any old plants that show signs of distorted leaves or blooms. To improve the risk of trouble-free plants, plant the bulbs as late in the year as possible, November or even later if you are prepared to chance the weather. The species tulips and the Darwin hybrids appear to be far more resistant to problems of deterioration so that is another alternative although very limiting in choice.

To reduce the risk of disease, plant tulips as late in the year as possible, November or even later, if the weather remains good.

In specialist catalogues, tulips are classified into a number of different categories which can be rather confusing. All you need to take into consideration when ordering is the height, shape and colour of the flower and the time of flowering. Try any of these reliable single varieties or just select your own but remember to discard varieties that don't live up to your expectations:

- 'Apricot Beauty' is an early variety with blooms of a good colour that last longer than most others, height 40cm, late April;
- 'Bellona' is a yellow version of 'Apricot Beauty', a little earlier and only 30cm high;
- 'Purple Prince' is the same height and flowers at the same time as 'Bellona'
- 'Bing Crosby' is a good scarlet tulip flowering at the end of April, height 40cm;
- 'Grand Perfection' is a variety reminiscent of those depicted in oils by the Dutch Old Masters with dark red and white streaked flowers in late April on 40cm stems;
- 'Hemisphere' has flowers ranging from white through pale pink to deep rose with every shade and streak in between, so they look wonderful when

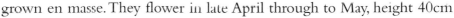

grown en masse. They flower in late April through to May, height 40cm

- For pure white try 'Pax', 40cm high, flowering in early May;
- 'Apeldoorn' is a tall, strong growing, Darwin hybrid tulip that appears to be more disease resistant than most, with large crimson flower heads open mid-April on 60cm stems;
- 'Queen of Night' is one of the most-loved tulips with maroon, almost black, single flowers. It looks good amongst other flower colours but the blooms can become lost in front of dark evergreens. A later flowering variety, opening in mid-May and 60cm tall;
- 'Spring Green' has unusual ivory blooms streaked with a broad band of green. It is invaluable as a cut flower and is good in pots or borders. It flowers during April at a height of 50cm;
- 'Esperanto' has flowers which are also streaked with green, this time on a deep rose base. The leaves are variegated with a cream edge, a combination that really only works well in pots or in contemporary borders when placed amongst brooding, dark foliage;
- 'White Triumphator' and 'Marilyn' are both tall lily-flowered tulips, very refined and they look their best in formal borders or when grown for use as cut flowers. Somehow their elegance looks out of place elsewhere. Both flower in early May. Both are white although 'Marilyn' is streaked with red.

The double-flowered tulips are very beautiful when grown well but invariably they get knocked and battered by the changeable spring weather. They can develop to perfection in an unheated greenhouse, planted direct in the ground or in large pots and used as cut flowers. Try 'Black Parrot', a deep, fluffy-looking maroon and 'White Parrot' – both are stunning. 'Angelique' is another double, pale pink that when fully open looks more like a peony than a tulip. In the garden they all flower mid-May; in the greenhouse, probably two or three weeks earlier.

Once you start experimenting with growing the tulip species, you are likely to want to try more and more different varieties because of their simple charm and beauty. *Tulipa hageri* 'Splendens' is a deep velvety red, 20cm tall and flowering in April. Tulipa 'Peppermint Stick' has small pointed blooms, the colour of seaside rock, pink on the outside and white on the inside – try cramming an outdoor pot full of them for a dazzling effect in late March. *Tulipa sylvestris* can be found growing wild in England but is very rare and protected. Small, pale yellow and very scented flowers appear in the garden during March.

CHAPTER FIVE

Soil Without Toil

Giving your plants the best growing conditions

To get the most pleasure from your garden you need to know what you enjoy doing and what you don't and this will vary from person to person. Cultivation of the soil is one of those tasks that you either love or hate but it is an essential process if you are to give your plants the best start in life. If the thought of digging is too awful to contemplate then it may be necessary to employ an outside contractor to carry out the initial preparation or to adjust your garden plan to minimise it. Once the initial preparation has been completed, further major digging can be kept to an absolute minimum or often avoided altogether.

How to know your soil type
Sandy, clay – or just perfect?

As a rule of thumb, the longer a plant is going to remain in place the greater the need for good soil conditions and the more care and time you need to take with planting. The first consideration is what type of soil you have and this can be quite confusing – and dull – if you are not a soil enthusiast. You do not need to know the technical terms for the different sorts of soil; all you have to do is to go into the garden with a fork and try to push it into the ground. Different parts of the garden can dig quite differently to others parts so do this test wherever you are planning to grow things. Obviously if the weather has been hot and dry for weeks this will be more difficult, but assuming normal weather conditions how easy are you finding it to do this? Strength also plays a part, of course, but it is just as important to get the soil right for *you* to be able to work it easily as it is for your plants to be able to grow well in it. In the perfect world, the fork will go readily into nice, crumbly, rich brown earth but all too often this is not the case.

If the soil is hard and cracks appear on its surface soon after warm, dry weather starts or is sticky and lumpy after rain, you almost certainly will be gardening on clay. Depending on just how high the clay content is, this can be a tricky soil to get to the desired texture for the number of days in the year when it is perfect for digging can be few. However, a clay soil has a number of advantages too, for it holds water and nutrients well to the plants' benefit and once it has been dug there are ways to make it easier (page 104).

Perhaps your fork has gone into fine earth that is quite crumbly and dry. If this is happening after rain then you will have a free-draining soil which although easier to work may suffer more frequently from drought and loss of nutrients. Again, there are straightforward ways to avoid some of these issues.

Next, pick up a small amount of soil in your hand and try rolling a pinch of it between your finger and thumb to make a pea-sized ball. If the ball forms easily and ends up feeling like putty or Blu-Tack it has a high clay content, often described as 'heavy' soil; if it feels gritty and keeps falling apart then you have what is termed 'light' soil. Samples that form a ball which break up readily mean you have the easiest soil conditions for gardening in.

How to tell if your soil is acid or alkaline

You cannot tell just by staring at or feeling the soil whether it is acid or alkaline; these are words that often confuse, especially when talked about in terms of the pH scale quoted in some manuals. A soil pH of 7 is perfectly balanced or neutral; above this figure the soil becomes increasingly alkaline and below it, increasingly acid. This balance will have a direct effect on how plants thrive but fortunately the majority of them tolerate a wide range of conditions.

It isn't necessary to know the pH value of your soil, although you can buy a testing kit if you wish – most gardeners just talk about their soil either being acidic/peaty or alkaline/chalky/limey, if they talk of it at all. Some plants do require acid conditions to grow well and if you see rhododendrons, summer-flowering heathers, blue-flowered hydrangeas (they turn pink in alkaline soil) in your neighbours' gardens these are all indicators of your soil type.

It is very difficult to successfully change the pH of your soil and one of the differences that will make your garden a great one is to choose plants that thrive in your soil type. Check the labels of plants as you buy them and don't plant something that requires damp, acidic soil somewhere dry and with a high alkaline content, for it will be only a matter of time before it looks poorly.

Digging and how to avoid it

One of the most common mistakes with digging is digging too deeply and too much. The old gardening manuals are full of techniques and terms such as double digging, a back-breaking procedure enough to deter even the keenest of gardeners. Often it results in the nutrients that are found close to the surface of the soil being buried beneath cloddy subsoil. Even more often, it ends in injury and another person put off gardening for life.

Consider what you are trying to achieve – are you planting a tree or a flower border? If the latter then you will need to fork over the whole area; if it is a tree then all that is required is a well dug planting hole. Even in the border there may be some areas that do not need to be dug as deeply as others: shrubs will want deeper soil preparation than small herbaceous plants. Be guided by your common sense but don't be tempted to skimp with it for the results will inevitably be disappointing.

The technique of digging is a difficult one to describe and you will soon find your own style that suits you best. Don't try to lift or turn as big a piece of earth as possible for this will result in back strain and tiredness; taking smaller 'bites' is easier and you will be able to continue working for longer. The lumps of soil also break up more readily creating a finer surface ('tilth' in garden jargon terms).

If you are starting a new bed or extending one in what has previously been lawn, mow the grass as short as possible before starting to dig as this will make it considerably easier to work with. You may prefer to remove the grass altogether and for this a mattock is an invaluable tool as it keeps your back straight, whereas a spade can make it a very tiring and uncomfortable task. For larger areas still, it is possible to hire a turf-lifting machine which is very straightforward to use.

Sometimes you can avoid digging altogether which is especially the case if you are planting a shrub border. If previously grass, mow it short as described and then spray the area with Roundup, a contact herbicide which does not leave a residue in the soil. After a fortnight you will be able to dig planting holes for the individual shrubs and plant them as normal. The remaining unplanted areas can be covered with a mulch to minimise weed growth. Mulches are discussed in more detail on pages 104–105.

Vegetable gardens and allotments

In larger gardens one of the areas that require constant attention is the vegetable garden and all too frequently it becomes weed infested and unattractive. Often this is due to lack of time, a change in circumstances or advancing years making the physical labour more difficult. Sometimes it is best to admit defeat and grass the whole area over which then releases time for other parts of the garden. However, if growing vegetables is still important to you consider converting the garden to a series of raised beds, sometimes referred to as deep beds. Raised beds also work well on allotments.

Raised beds are easily made and even easier to maintain

The beds are easier to maintain if they have a raised edging and the timber boards used at the base of fence panels are ideal as they are treated to minimise decay and so last for a number of years. The beds are usually made one or two boards high; they can be even more raised than this if required although they will then need stronger corner posts and more frequent strengthening posts along their length. Use 7.5 x 7.5cm (3 x 3in) square fence posts for this, cut into sections and driven into the ground, then attach the boards to them, screws being stronger than nails. All the materials can be readily purchased from a builder's merchant or DIY store and only very basic skills are required to make them.

Don't make the beds too large for you will want to be able to reach their middle comfortably from the sides without standing on them. Likewise, they don't want to be too long or you will be tempted to take a shortcut across them rather than walk around. Leave paths between the beds that are wide enough to be able to work from comfortably and move a wheelbarrow down them if you have one. This may seem rather a waste of valuable growing space but you will find that you can grow your vegetables at very much closer intervals in a raised bed so little is actually lost in real terms.

If you make your raised beds a regular size, e.g. 10 square metres, it makes it easier to calculate rates for sowing seeds or fertilising.

There are two ways of filling your raised beds. The obvious one is to import topsoil and fill them which can be expensive, time consuming and jolly hard work. The other is to dig down into the soil and fit the boards so that they are buried to half their depth. Once that is done you then dig out the paths, throwing the soil onto the raised beds until the boards are exposed once again. The boards can then be secured easily.

This may all sound like a lot of hard work and, of course, it is, but it will save you a lot of time in the long term and give you an area that is very productive, easy to work and to be proud of. Raised beds also warm up quicker in the spring giving earlier crops because they drain freely which means that you can work them even after rain, a great advantage when gardening on clay soils.

Once all the beds have been made – and you may consider paying someone to do it – they are dug over thoroughly and, here is the point, they are not dug deeply or walked on ever again. Maintenance is carried out from the sides and any cultivation is limited to preparation for planting or seed sowing.

If you decide to grass the paths over do make sure that they are wide enough for your mower to travel down easily. It will also be worthwhile investing in a strimmer to prevent the grass from growing untidily around the board edges which, if left, will prevent your garden looking good.

It is possible to create raised beds without the timber boards which will give them a rounded appearance. However, maintenance is more time consuming as weed growth constantly encroaches from the paths.

Getting your soil right

The more you garden the more instinctive you will become about its requirements and nowhere is this truer than when it comes to soil. You will very quickly know which parts of the garden are easy to work and which need more attention.

The more you work with your soil the greater the improvement in its quality but this does not mean that you have to be constantly digging it.

It is very easy to improve both soil texture and fertility through the use of mulches and composts placed on the surface which are then drawn into the soil by worm activity or through weathering. They also help conserve moisture within the soil so are especially useful on light, free-draining ones.

Composts and mulches – what are they?

The difference between compost and mulch is that composts are often dug into the soil; mulches are always spread across the surface of it. Whereas all composts can be used as mulches, not all mulches are dug into the ground although they are often absorbed into it as they rot or as maintenance procedures take place.

A note on potting compost

The bags sold in garden centres rather confusingly as potting compost are different to the types of compost described here – they are used specifically for growing plants or for sowing seeds in pots and containers. There is no reason, however, why you can't dispose of old or unwanted potting compost by spreading it thinly on your borders.

The different types of composts and mulches for general use in the garden

Types of compost

Name	Source	Do I use it as a compost or a mulch?
Garden compost	It's free if you make it at home	Either – it can be dug into the ground or left on the surface
Green waste	Garden centres	Either – use in the same way as garden compost but more sparingly
Mushroom compost	Garden centres Mushroom farms Small ads	Mulch – but only because it is rather costly. Rich and heavy, it is ideal for using on exposed sites where a lighter mulch when dry might blow away. It can be rather smelly when wet so use with caution near the house. Do not use on plants such as rhododendrons that dislike lime
Grass cuttings	Free	Mulch – it can be laid thickly at the foot of hedges or raspberry canes, ideally over a generous layer of damp newspaper to make a weed-proof barrier. More often it is added as an ingredient of the garden compost heap or mixed with leaves to make leaf mould
Straw	Local farms	Mulch – traditionally used to lift ripening strawberry fruits off the ground. It can also be mixed with grass cuttings to improve the balance of garden compost heaps or placed over the crowns of plants that need protection from cold during the winter
Leaf mould	Free if homemade	Mulch – use around trees and shrubs unless you have a plentiful supply when you can use it everywhere
Chipped bark	Garden centres	Mulch – can be used as a weed-suppressing mulch around shrubs and trees, or to make informal paths. Buy special play grade bark which is less likely to splinter for children's play areas
Gravel	Garden centres DIY stores Builders merchants	Mulch – for paths and gravel gardens use a locally sourced stone if possible for cheaper freight costs. Place a layer of horticultural grade grit (bought from garden centres) at the base of pots to improve drainage and stability

How to make your own garden compost

However small your garden is, it is always worth making your own compost for although most, if not all, councils now have a green waste disposal service why give it away when it can become something so beneficial? Not only is it free, it helps the environment and is one of the best food sources for your soil.

The different types of compost bins

There are a number of different compost bins on the market and these can be purchased quite cheaply or even found on giveaway internet sites such as Freecycle. Usually these are made of plastic and are completely sealed apart from their lids and base which if stood on a stone slab makes them completely rat proof if this should be a concern of yours. Rats, incidentally, don't like disturbance so if you place your bin near to the house and visit it regularly you are far less likely to have problems. The main attractor to rats

Only the most rudimentary carpentry skills are needed to make these large compost bins

is inappropriate materials being put in compost bins such as cooked foods, meat scraps, bread, etc.

It is also easy to make your own compost bins using old pallets or the same timber boards and posts used in the making of raised beds. Contrary to popular belief, compost bins are better if they do not have gaps or holes for air to enter their sides so, if using pallets, line the sides with old cardboard cartons – these will rot down and be a useful addition to the compost.

If you have a large garden you may find it useful to have a number of bins either placed side by side or put singly in strategic places.

What can I use to make garden compost?

The answer is pretty much what you want apart from those already mentioned above. Other items to avoid are cat and dog litter and/or faeces, manmade fibres, plastics, polystyrene and disposable nappies. Garden waste materials to avoid adding to your heaps are thick branches which take forever to rot, any plants that have running roots such as ground elder and anything with thorns – these aren't detrimental but the thorns take a very long time to rot and continue to spear you making life unpleasant. Evergreen leaves are also best left out of the heaps for they will take a long time to rot unless they have been passed through a garden shredder first.

Compost-making manuals can make the whole procedure sound very complicated, time consuming and hard work. Turning your heaps, which involves digging them out and putting them back in reverse order so that the bottom of the heap becomes the top, does speed up the decaying process but is quite an unnecessary chore if you're prepared to wait a bit longer for the finished result.

The secret to successful compost making is to have a good mix of materials; these heat up and with the combination of worms, warmth and (friendly) bacteria they rot down to produce a crumbly, rich and highly nutritious plant feed. How long does it take? It can vary but can be as quick as 12 weeks although it usually takes longer.

Table 4 provides a list of some of the ingredients you can put into your heap. It is not necessary to remember them all and it is easier to think of them just as 'greens' and 'browns', the latter being anything that once was derived from plants but now do not have any leaves.

Table 4: Garden compost

Greens	Browns
Weeds (but not those with troublesome roots)	Twigs and small branches (broken up)
Hedge clippings (not evergreens unless first shredded)	Newspaper (crumpled)
	Shredded paper waste
Garden plant trimmings	Cardboard (crumpled)
Vegetable garden waste	Toilet rolls
Uncooked kitchen waste (not meat)	Cardboard egg cartons
Fruit	Small animal pet bedding
Grass clippings (but see note below)	Straw (in small quantities)
	Egg shells
	Leaves (but see note below)

Ideally you will make up the compost heaps in alternate layers of greens and browns, the latter allow plenty of air to circulate within the compost which speeds up the process. Although the end product should have a rich Christmas pudding texture, it is not an exact science and so you do not need worry unduly about it. There may well be parts of it that have not broken down as much as you would have hoped and these can be used to start the new compost bin off.

What can I do with all my grass clippings?

In summer, there can be so many grass clippings from mowing that the compost heap becomes overwhelmed with it, resulting in a slimy, rank-smelling heap. If possible, increase the amount of 'browns' to compensate, although it can be hard to find enough if you have a large area of lawn being mown each week. One way to avoid this is to use the clippings as a moisture-retaining mulch at the foot of raspberry canes or hedges. They should be laid quite thickly, preferably with a good layer of newspaper beneath them and starting when the soil is already damp.

An alternative use of them if you have a separate leaf heap (see below) is to make alternate layers of grass and leaves ('greens' and 'browns'). This will resolve the problem of the grass and speed the rotting of the leaves to their mutual benefit.

If your garden compost looks too wet add more 'browns' to it; if it is too dry and not rotting add more 'greens'.

If neither of these options are possible, a last resort may be to dispose of some of the clippings in the council bins for municipal recycling.

How can I put all my autumn leaves to good use?

If you have a large number of trees knowing what to do with all of the dropped leaves can become an issue. Apart from adding them to lawn clippings there are other ways of disposing of them without resorting to bonfires. If you have relatively few leaves falling in your garden it is best to add them as shallow layers to your compost heap. If you have more the best option is to make a separate heap.

Unlike garden compost, leaves only need to be contained in a wire mesh enclosure to prevent them from being blown around. They can stay there for as long as it takes them to rot down to a beautiful, rich, crumbly mix, a process that may take up to two years. It does not matter if there are pieces of leaf still showing, it is ready for use as soon as there is no chance of it blowing around.

A simple way of making small quantities of leaf mould is to fill black plastic dustbin liners with dampened leaves. Tie the tops in a knot, place them somewhere where they can lie undisturbed and puncture the bags a few times with a garden fork.

Leaf mould, as the resulting compost is known, is the perfect and natural plant food to place around your trees and shrubs in the autumn. Any spring bulbs that are buried beneath them will push through it quite happily but avoid covering the crowns of any other flowering plants that may be there.

How to take good care of yourself

If you have ever suffered from back pain or have any sort of allergy or heart condition it does not necessarily mean that you cannot garden. The growing popularity of 'green gyms' is evidence of the health benefits that can be derived from physical activity in the open air. However, it is important to discuss any concerns you may have with your doctor and there are also ways to help yourself avoid future problems.

Get into the habit of thinking through every task, asking constantly how you can make this easier, for your health is your most precious asset and you must protect yourself from injury, the majority of which can always be foreseen.

Most health problems occur when no gardening has been carried out for some time and, with a sudden fit of enthusiasm, you try and do too much too quickly.

Digging and other strenuous work should be kept to a minimum and it may be worth considering employing someone to do this for you, especially if you are short of time. Quite often, strain injuries occur because the tools being used, whatever they are, are too short or too long in the handle or too heavy; other times because the technique in using them is wrong. See page 179 for specific advice on using tools safely.

Stepping onto an upturned rake left lying on the ground, only to be knocked unconscious by the handle as it flies up and hits you on the forehead, may be an old slapstick joke but it is one of the most common garden injuries. Always stand a rake or any other long-handled tool upright so that this cannot happen.

Tripping is another frequently encountered hazard, again usually caused by tools left lying around but also sometimes by hosepipes. Consider buying one that is bright yellow rather than green for they show up well – whatever their colour they should be safely coiled away when not in use if you want your garden to look good.

Lifting heavy weights is a great cause of back problems and it is never wise to attempt anything that cannot be moved easily without good reason. Shop-bought composts can be purchased in different size bags or, if necessary, tip some out into a spare bag before lifting. Wheelbarrows should not be overloaded, a useful ploy when weeding as frequent emptying will make you stand up and walk a few yards, straightening and easing your back which is beneficial whether you suffer from pain or not.

Not all injuries occur because of gardening, of course; some health problems are of long standing. If bending or general mobility is a problem, obviously many tasks will be difficult and assistance may be needed or you may find raised borders and some of the lightweight, long-reach tools help. There is no reason why you should not be able to still derive great pleasure from being in control of your garden and to proudly claim it as your own just because you cannot manage all of the tasks.

CHAPTER SIX

Maintenance – How to Enjoy it

No matter how clever you are at design, colour scheming or plant naming if your garden isn't well maintained it will never look good or give you the full degree of pleasure that you are striving for. No-one ever asks the question, 'Why can't my garden look like that?' when there are weed-filled borders, unkempt lawns and worn-out paths to be seen. The key answer to having a beautiful garden is maintenance, but that doesn't mean that you have to spend every spare moment of your time doing it. There are a number of shortcuts that can be learnt and you will probably discover some of your own that suit you and your garden.

A well-maintained garden can mean many different things to different people. For some it will mean everything is manicured and clipped and brushed to an inch of its life, for others it means a much more relaxed approach giving the garden a natural feel. One of the most common mistakes with those that want the latter is thinking that nature will take care of itself; the best 'wild' gardens are carefully managed with the skill of the gardener evident by the lack of obvious interference.

Try to work regularly in the garden. The tasks are not as great or time consuming as when they are left for longer and, as a consequence, you will enjoy them more and have a greater feeling of satisfaction.

Two of the biggest questions that you needed to answer honestly at the beginning of the review process were how much time are you able to devote to the garden and just how much you actually like and want to do it. If everything you have done so far has been carried out with these two answers always in mind, there should be few problems with on-going maintenance. Of course, the best plans can go awry with sudden crises arising but gardening is not an exact art and it may not matter all that much if some tasks are missed out for a season or two. The secret to having a garden that appears to be beautifully maintained is to prioritise the work and this may not necessarily be in the order that you might expect.

Top 10 'must do' tasks for a quick maintenance makeover

If the weather is awful, or there just aren't enough hours in the day to get outside for long, try to make sure that you do at least some of the following tasks. From a distance, the garden will still look well maintained.

1 Trim the lawn edges – it is surprising how even quite long grass instantly looks smarter and well cared for. Letting the edges of a lawn grow straggly, even when it is regularly mown, has the opposite effect.

2 Keep paths and driveways weed free – spraying regularly with herbicide stops the weeds from getting too large which means that they die without showing up. Large, dead weeds look even worse than large, alive weeds and will need to be physically removed, a tedious and time-consuming job.

3 Keep the front garden well maintained at all times, or at least the area that leads to the front door. It will be seen by visitors and by yourself every day of the year, whatever the weather.

4 Keep any pots and planters that are close to the house free of weeds, dead flowers removed and, if topiary, clipped. If you haven't time for that

A well-defined and neat lawn edge makes a huge difference to the overall appearance of the garden

and they look shabby, remove the pots altogether until you do have time to sort them out.

5 If you have bare soil you will have weeds. Keep any areas that you can easily see free from weeds. If you have very little time just pull out the tallest ones that show up from a distance.

6 Formal hedges of box or yew really do need to be kept beautifully maintained. Clip as often as necessary and consider removing them if you just can't manage their upkeep.

7 Deadhead flowers that are fading or chop down whole plants that look shabby – just one dead or dying plant in a key place can spoil the garden's whole appearance.

8 Prune shrubs and climbers that are getting out of control before they become too large – even if it means doing it 'out of season'. If a branch is in your way or a climber invading your window space or gutters, cut it back even if you leave the rest of the plant until you have more time.

9 Pressure wash or treat paths and steps that become slippery when wet. You must make time for this (or pay someone else to do it) before you fall. An injury will mean even less time available for gardening.

10 Remove fallen leaves from gravel paths, and ideally lawns and borders, as quickly and as often as possible. Buy or hire a leaf blower if raking is too tiring or time consuming. Leaving them to pile up might seem an easy option but may damage the grass – and once the earthworms start to pull the leaves into the ground it is far more difficult to remove them.

Working with the seasons

This is an oft-used phrase but what does it really mean? Foremost it is a way of saying use common sense. Garden books often give specific times for carrying out jobs but it is essential to consider what the weather is doing, not just right then but over the following few days and weeks. There is no point, for example, in sowing seeds into cold, wet soil when they may rot just because it is technically spring. Better to wait a few days or even a couple of weeks and carry out the task when the ground has had a chance to dry and warm up a little. Over time, you will instinctively know when to delay jobs or when to bring them forward and it is this learning process which makes gardening no longer a chore but a fascinating and absorbing hobby.

There are certain jobs that should be completed regardless of what the seasons are doing and the most important of these is the autumn tidy and cleaning up. Try to get all the herbaceous plants cut back (unless you are keeping them for decorative seed heads), borders weeded and leaves swept up by Christmas. The New Year often brings the first of prolonged winter weather making these jobs very difficult and there are often other things that can be done then anyway. The late garden designer and plantswoman, Rosemary Verey, described this job as 'putting the garden to bed for the winter' which describes it perfectly. Once you have completed this you can relax and breathe a sigh of relief, knowing that the garden is being given the very best chance for success the following year.

Spring

In some ways, in the gardening calendar, autumn ought to be considered the start of the year. However, convention tells us that Spring (March – May) is the first season and, besides, that is when most of us begin to think about working outside once again after the bleak months of January and February.

Spring is the time when the weather can be at its most changeable with warm, sometimes hot, days followed by cold, frosty nights. Damaging frosts can occur at any time during these months, often catching us unawares and setting the garden back. Don't be in a rush to plant out tender plants unless you are able to cover them over at night if a late frost is likely. Horticultural fleece or even newspapers laid lightly over the tops of them can often protect them and make all the difference between life and death.

Lawns

As the temperature rises and the days start to lengthen, grass begins to grow, slowly at first and then rapidly reaching a peak around midsummer before slowing down once again. Although mowing can very occasionally be carried out in mild winter months the start of the regular mowing regime usually begins in March. Begin with the blades of the mower set high, just cutting the tips off the grass for the first two or three mowings to avoid damaging it. Gradually, the blades can be lowered to the desired height for regular cutting. It is tempting to cut the grass very short to avoid having to do it as frequently but this is harmful to the grass for a number of reasons. It weakens it, allows weeds and moss to develop more readily and leaves the grass in poor condition to cope with drought. For the average lawn the grass during spring should be cut to a height of 2.5–4cm.

Stripes on a mown lawn always impress – but only if they are straight, which takes practice. They are formed not by the cutting action of the blades but by the roller behind them, so if you want stripes make sure your mower has one fitted.

Once the grass is growing actively, it can be treated with an all-round weed killer and fertiliser – it is important to use one that is specifically designed for lawns. Regular feeding and weeding is desirable if you want a good looking, healthy lawn and there are numerous companies that will come and do these jobs for you at reasonable costs, saving you both time or the need to buy or hire the necessary equipment. If you don't like the idea of using weed killers, like to see daisies or are not too fussy about the lawn, being satisfied if it just stays green, then that is fine too. In such cases, if large weeds like dandelions, thistles or docks are a problem, they can always be spot treated with weed killer or physically removed by cutting just below ground level – an old bread knife is admirable for this. They do regrow but gradually weaken if cut again.

Scarifying is another task that can be carried out once the grass is growing well. This is vigorous raking to remove the build-up of dead grass that forms at soil level (called 'thatch'). It also cuts the side roots of the grass making them grow more vigorously, a sort of below ground pruning. A special hand rake can be used for this process but, even with small lawns, it is a tiring and soul-destroying job: far better and easier to hire a scarifying machine or call in the lawn maintenance people to do this job for you.

Borders

All of the different sorts of borders described earlier – herbaceous, mixed, shrub, etc., can be included together here for their maintenance is very similar.

The spring-flowering bulbs may well have started to flower as early as January although the bulk of them bloom during the three spring months. Whether in flower or not, they will be showing well through the ground and many of the herbaceous plants will also be forming new shoots with the earliest sorts beginning to flower. It is a busy time of year in the garden for growth and even on a regular daily walk you will notice subtle changes taking place.

Weeds will be growing actively and now is the time to weed the borders just as thoroughly as you did in their final autumn tidy. Try not to stint on this first weeding for it will save you time in the longer term. Gradually, as the garden plants grow and fill the spaces, most weeds will be crowded out and, although weeding never stops completely, it does become less frenetic through the summer.

Some plants such as aquilegia and poppies are prolific self-seeders and these will be germinating now. If you come across seedling plants and you aren't certain whether they are weeds or not, let them grow on a bit until you can identify them.

As spring progresses and the soil warms up – you can feel the difference in temperature with your hand – any seeds that you want to sow can be planted now, marking them carefully with a label or stick as a reminder where they are. Many annual plants are very quick to grow and flower from seed and are excellent ways of filling in the gaps between newly planted herbaceous plants. Over time, the herbaceous plants will spread and fill these spaces but, by then, the annuals will have finished and can be removed.

In early spring, as soon as there are signs of new growth, the ornamental grasses (and those herbaceous plants that have retained their grass-like foliage through the winter) can have all their leaves trimmed back to a few inches above ground level. Some of the grasses form a low, raised mound or tussock and only need to be cut back to this. It is a very quick and worthwhile job as it keeps the plants looking fresh and tidy all summer – twist the leaves into a bunch in one hand and cut with the other, rather like cutting off a pony tail. A similar process should be carried out with ferns at the same time.

Unless you have the time to care for them, it is better not to grow plants that require staking to keep them upright. Your garden will never look good if your plants have fallen over just as they are coming into flower and they often look even worse if they are then gathered up and tied tightly to bamboo canes. To avoid this, buy sturdy self-supporting plants or shorter-growing varieties. An alternative, if the type of plant is suitable, is to give it the 'Chelsea chop' (see page 177). If you grow plants such as delphiniums and peonies they will almost certainly require staking, traditionally done with canes and balls of twine or cut hazel sticks. A quicker alternative is to purchase 'L' shaped, interconnecting stakes made of plastic-coated steel. These are robust, come in different heights, last for years and soon get hidden by the growing plant.

Tying plants up too tightly to prevent toppling can make them look very ugly

---

Fit supports if you are using them before the plants grow too large and actually require them. The result will be natural-looking plants as the supports will have disappeared from view beneath the foliage.

Bulbs

Many of the spring-flowering bulbs require little or no maintenance whatsoever and will continue to flower and increase in number year after year. This is especially true of the smaller varieties such as crocus, snowdrops and grape hyacinths. It is part of their annual cycle for their leaves to wither and die immediately after flowering, the bulb becoming dormant until regrowth starts again in the autumn.

Daffodil leaves, especially of the more robust varieties, take longer to die and can look quite ugly at the front of borders. If possible, tuck them under the new foliage of other plants to die off naturally unseen. To maintain vigour in the bulb, remove the flower stalk immediately the flower dies, if you do this at ground level the plant will look tidier. It is important never to pull the flower stalk away from the bulb: always cut it. If you have daffodils growing in grass, the leaves can look quite unsightly but do not be tempted

Spring bulbs always look best when grouped in quantity

to cut them off or mow over them for six weeks after flowering as this does not allow the bulb to absorb nutrients from the dying leaves. If growing in this way, it is beneficial to feed daffodils immediately after flowering with an autumn lawn feed but do make sure that it does not contain weed killers.

Tulips should be rigorously deadheaded and any fallen petals removed for these often carry the diseases that make the bulbs deteriorate in following years. However, we rarely have the time to do this and it is usually better to consider tulips as short-lived bulbs that require replacing from time to time.

Trees and shrubs

As the season progresses more and more will be coming into leaf and flowering. As their flowers fade, some may require pruning to keep them in shape or to restrict their size. See page 162 for specific details.

Roses will need spraying regularly, once a fortnight, throughout the summer if you are to keep diseases such as rust and blackspot at bay. If you buy a spray that is combined with a pesticide it will kill insect pests such as aphids at the same time but it will kill off, of course, all the beneficial insects too. Any pruning of rose bushes should be completed during April.

Roses when kept pest and disease free can look stunning

Climbers

The *montana* clematis can be clipped hard back after flowering although this is not an essential task. When not done, however, the plants become ever larger with a great deal of unsightly dead wood.

As climbers send out new shoots any that are heading off in the wrong direction can be tucked in or tied to their supporting frame, or failing that, cut back.

Sweet peas are easy to grow from seed sown either in the autumn or spring, or young plants can be purchased. These can be planted out either in the border or in the cutting garden but will need to be given 1.8m supports to climb up. In the border, twiggy branches or bought pyramids or obelisks where the plants can grow naturally look best. If grown specifically for cutting, lines of bamboo canes similar to those for growing runner beans are more orderly and easier to maintain.

Summer

The changeable weather of spring has given way to day after day of hot, dry, summer days — at least, that's the theory. Although frost is still possible in June it is rare and most plants are now thriving with the increase in temperature and the long daylight hours. Take advantage of the longer days to spend time in the garden, enjoying the fruits of your labours and taking notes or photographs of areas that you think are working really well or those that need some adjusting.

Prolonged dry spells can cause problems for plants, especially newly planted ones and those in pots, and regular watering may prove necessary.

These shallow baskets of house leeks rarely require watering and look just as good when covered in frost

Lawns

Mowing will now become a weekly task; try not to leave it to get too long for a nicely mown lawn, even if not of the best quality, really does make a huge difference to the appearance of your garden.

Weed killing and feeding can continue right through the summer, usually once a month, but this does not preclude you from doing it just on an occasional basis if you just can't find the time.

If grass cutting is taking too long consider letting some of it grow longer, perhaps allowing wild flowers to thrive. Give the area some cohesion by mowing a path through or around it. If leaving it to grow long and unkempt doesn't appeal, cut this longer grass on the highest setting of the mower which saves time and gives the garden yet another, different green texture. This works especially well under trees where shorter mown grass may struggle to grow well.

By August the grass will, in the average summer, have slowed down and, although it will still need regular mowing the amount of clippings and the time it takes will be reduced.

In dry periods, especially if it is hot, the lawn (unless regularly watered) can turn quite brown and scorched but will soon green up again after rain. Grass growth will be much reduced or stop completely but weeds, which cope better with these conditions, are likely to continue to grow. Mowing now will be purely to keep these under control to prevent the lawns looking too untidy.

During hot, dry periods raising the height of your mower blades will help keep the lawns looking green and healthy. The shorter you cut your grass, the more prone it will be to stress at times of drought.

Borders

The borders will be flowering at their peak during the summer months and tasks will be limited to removing dead flower heads to encourage further flowering and improve the plants' appearance. Some, such as lady's mantle, geraniums and catmint can be cut back to ground level as their first flowers fade which will encourage new, fresh leaves and flowers to develop.

If the borders are full, there will be little bare soil showing and weed growth will be minimalised but those that do appear should be removed. During dry spells, working these spaces with a hoe (see page 180) is a quick

Delphiniums are dominant in this well stocked and colourful summer border

method of control but only if they haven't grown too large.

Staking and tying-in of plants that are collapsing should continue to be carried out where it is proving necessary.

By August, many of the earlier flowering plants will have come to an end despite your best endeavours and it is important that you have included some of the later flowering plants to extend interest through to late autumn. Many of the taller daisies are good for this – rudbeckia, aster, echinacea and helenium will all bloom right through to the first frosts. Dahlia, too, bloom from midsummer onwards but these will require digging out and storing somewhere frost-free to overwinter or, easier still, replace each year with new.

Bulbs

The majority of bulbs planted in gardens flower in spring but there are some that bloom during the summer months. Most of the alliums flower during May and June, lilies start midsummer as do gladioli. Although the latter are difficult to include in the flower border, their stiff upright growth and exotic colours often looking out of place, they make terrific cut flowers so are

126

sometimes best grown specifically for that purpose. However, they do associate well with some of the taller grasses – for an explosion of colour try growing them amongst these and *Verbena bonariensis*.

August will see the first flowers of the autumn bulbs such as crocus, cyclamen and colchicum. The buds show before their leaves start to grow so, if planted in grass, be careful not to mow them off.

Trees and shrubs

There will be little to do other than occasional pruning which is covered in more detail in Chapter 8.

Hedges, especially formal, evergreen ones such as box and yew, and topiary, will need regular clipping from June onwards as it is important that these are well maintained if you want your garden to look good. It is better to dispense with them altogether if you do not have the time or patience to keep these formal hedges looking neat and precise. Other evergreen shrubs should be pruned during midsummer too.

As August is a relatively quiet month in the garden, it is also a good time to cut other hedges although it is sometimes easier to find the time during the winter. The task will be out of the way before the busier autumn period and birds should have finished nesting too. The prunings, if small, can be added to the compost heap, but bulkier ones or thorn-covered ones are best burnt, their ashes spread on the garden, or placed in the council bins for industrial-scale composting.

The summer pruning of apples and pears takes place when the topmost leaf opens, always the last to do so. Pruning at this time stimulates the buds encouraging fruiting, whereas winter pruning may create a greater volume of new growth. It is a good habit to get into but is not one of those essential jobs if you are short of time.

Climbers

Little needs doing with these other than continuing to train new growth into place. Sweet peas need to be picked regularly if they are to continue blooming.

Honeysuckle often gets covered in a white dust (powdery mildew), their leaves drying up and falling off, especially when grown against walls. This usually happens as the flowers are finishing. Cut the flowering branches hard back to within a couple of new pairs of buds which will now be visible as tiny red points close to the stems. As honeysuckle flowers on new growth, the plants will be unaffected and their general appearance improved. Like so many tasks in the garden it is not essential to do this but if done each year it is quite a quick job and prevents the plants from becoming a tangle of dead and living branches.

Wisterias send out huge volumes of growth every year and often this is left to grow unchecked until it becomes a major issue. Cut back any of the long tendrils by half to prevent them from becoming entwined with one another. Try not to miss out on this summer pruning although, all too often, this does happen. They will require a more severe pruning in winter regardless of whether you have done this summer task or not.

Autumn

In good years, September and October can be warm pleasant months to be outside in the garden although shortening daylight will give less time. Many of the flowering plants survive the first few frosts but there comes the day when all the blooms and, often the leaves too, are destroyed. This is the time to start the autumn tidy, perhaps the most important time for creating a garden with real 'wow' factor for lack of order now can have long-reaching consequences.

The leaves of *Viburnum opulus* turn crimson in autumn before falling

Autumn is also the time of year when the soil is warm and usually quite moist, perfect for planting new plants and moving more established ones.

Leaves will be turning beautiful colours not just on the trees and shrubs but also on some of the herbaceous plants too. These colours, however stunning, are all too short-lived and it is important not to become too focused on planting just for autumn colour when selecting plants for the garden.

Lawns

Mowing will continue throughout this period but gradually will become less frequent. The blades should be raised slightly so that the grass does not have to cope with harsh, winter weather cut too short.

Feeding the lawn with summer fertilisers must be stopped as they promote soft, sappy growth that will not stand up to wintry conditions well. Instead, feed in September or October with a low nitrogen autumn fertiliser which strengthens the lawn grasses. Often this fertiliser incorporates a moss killer too which will turn black as it dies; once this happens it should be scarified out.

If your lawn is poorly drained or the soil over compacted it may be worthwhile aerating the grass with a hollow tine aerator which takes out a core of earth, leaving holes that allow air, water and fertilisers to stimulate the soil and roots. Many books show this task being done by hand – or rather foot – with a garden fork, a tedious and demoralising task even in a tiny area, and of limited benefit unless done thoroughly. Don't waste valuable time doing this but hire a machine or the lawn care people to do all the hard work.

Leaves falling from surrounding trees will be a constant factor, and although tempting to leave on the grass, they encourage fungal growth and weaken it. If your mower has a grass collection box and can cope, pick them up with this, the blades set high – the chopping action will hasten the leaves' decay when composted and save a lot of time raking or blowing them off the grass.

Keep off the grass when heavily frosted as the footprints left will have damaged the grass blades, which when thawed out turn brown and will remain as unsightly reminders, often for many weeks.

Borders

The majority of herbaceous plants die back to ground or below ground level as the autumn progresses. This is part of their natural cycle and they will regrow in the spring stimulated by increasing daylight and warmth. As the plants become frosted and die back, cut down any unsightly growth to within a few inches of the ground; this can be added to the compost heap.

Some plants have decorative seedheads or desiccated foliage that can be left for continued winter interest. They are often visited by wild birds as a food source.

Leaves will be falling on the borders and these should also be removed regularly for they will harbour slugs and prevent the garden from looking good. If the borders are devoted purely to shrubs, trees and spring bulbs they can be left in place, saving time. However, during dry, windy periods they may blow around the garden creating additional more lengthy work later on.

Once the leaves are cleared the whole border should be forked over lightly, removing weeds. After this has been done, any plants that are performing poorly through overcrowding can be dug out, split up and some

Decorative seedheads can give added winter interest and provide food for wildlife

replanted as described on pages 50 and 52; those not required can be given away or planted elsewhere. Likewise, any plants that are growing in the wrong place can be removed now – disliked plants should always be removed immediately regardless of the season.

Bulbs

Autumn is the time for planting the majority of bulbs. Daffodils should be planted as soon as they become available although, in practice, this is often impossible as other flowering plants are still in full glory or the ground to hard and dry. In practice, October is often the most convenient month for planting – whatever the number of other tasks there are to do make sure that your bulbs (except tulips which are best planted in November) are in the ground before the leaves begin to fall. This is purely for practical reasons: leaf clearing can be a time-consuming task, leaving little room for bulb planting, although that should be given precedence if need be.

Daffodils look impressive when planted en masse edging a driveway –

A mowing strip free of bulbs adjacent to a driveway improves its appearance

but only when they are in flower. Their dying foliage will hang around for six weeks after flowering before it can be removed. If you have the space and they are growing in grass, set them back from the edge by at least two or three mower widths. You will then be able to keep the edge neatly mown which will counterbalance the untidiness of the dying leaves. You can never have too many daffodils elsewhere in the garden either but do remember to keep the stronger growing types towards the back of borders where they will show up just as well.

The majority of bulbs should be planted to a depth equal to twice the height of the bulb. This can sometimes be difficult to achieve and some bulbs will literally pull themselves down by their roots which is why it can be so difficult to find even quite large bulbs when digging out some years later.

If you want your bulbs to look as if they have been growing in place for years it is important to plant them in a naturalistic way. Take a handful of bulbs and half throw, half roll them across the ground with a similar action as when playing ten-pin bowling. Plant them where they land: you will find that some cluster closer than the recommended spacing and others are further apart. This method is also quite useful for linking different colours of the same bulb but where you don't want a hard dividing line between them: carry out the procedure with a mixture of the bulbs in the central section.

This rolling is best done only with certain bulbs such as daffodils and crocus, as many small bulbs are dark skinned and will be impossible to find amongst the grass blades or leaf litter. Even with the larger bulbs it is a good idea, if planting in grass, to mow it as short as possible first.

It doesn't just take skill to have bulbs in flower in pots for the home over Christmas, it also takes a degree of luck. Often hyacinths will stubbornly refuse to flower until early January but are no less lovely for that. The way to have a basket of three or more equally sized blooms is to grow more than that number individually. Select those that are required and transplant into the container or just hide the rims of the pots with moss, which should be purchased from a garden centre rather than collected from the wild.

The early flowering, multi-headed and very fragrant narcissi, often a variety called Paperwhite, are very easy to grow indoors. Their bulbs do not even need to go into soil but can just be supported using gravel. Paperwhite are good for planting in pots in the garden, especially by the front door, where their early blooms and scent will be most appreciated. They rarely succeed in the open garden and the bulbs are best discarded after blooming.

Trees and shrubs

Leaf fall is the natural progression from autumn to winter and even just a few mature trees can produce an awful lot of leaves that really ought to be cleared up to prevent damage to lawns and to smaller plants.

Raking is the easiest method if you only have very few to deal with; for more than this it may be worthwhile investing in a leaf blower (see page 185). Whichever way you collect them up they should be heaped either separately or mixed with other garden waste to produce one of the best free composts available.

Not all leaves decompose at the same rate and large evergreen leaves, unless shredded first, take for ever so are best burnt if you cannot do this. Holly leaves should always be burnt or sent to the municipal dump as their spines, just like thorns, remain long after the rest of the plant has decomposed, making handling it an uncomfortable and painful process.

Like other plants, trees and shrubs when planted at this time of year will establish quickly in the warm, moist soil.

Climbers

There is very little to do during this season except to remove any finished annual climbers such as sweet peas which can be dug up and thrown onto the compost heap. The perennial sweet pea which has smaller, unscented flowers does, as its name implies, die back to its roots to regrow the following spring. Its top growth can also be removed now.

Planting of new climbers can take place.

Winter

Although the days are short, the weather at this time of year can be remarkably changeable with relatively milder days interspersed with crisp, cold, sunny ones. Unless snow is lying on the ground there are still things that can be done in the garden, although the degree of urgency is over.

When you are stuck indoors because of the weather take time to stand at the windows and look at the garden, analysing what you see. When it is frosty or snow-covered the garden takes on a completely new appearance with outlines and structures dominating, unsoftened by summer flowers and foliage. It is now that much of what you have been working towards will prove worthwhile for the garden will still be attractive and interesting, albeit in a different way. Although there will no doubt be certain things that you want to

The garden in winter is transformed by heavy frost

change, or don't feel have worked as well as you might have hoped, it is important that you recognise the huge improvements that you have made.

Cold, wintry days are also useful for staying indoors and looking at plant and seed catalogues, reading up on new ideas for, as your knowledge and successes expand, so will your thirst for more information.

Lawns

It is possible in milder periods to run over the lawn with the mower blades set high during any of the winter months. This isn't to try and cut the grass as such, more to keep it looking tidy and clear of debris – you will be surprised at the difference to the lawn's appearance this will make. The grass needs to be dry too, a combination of weather conditions that are rare at this time of year for usually dry conditions mean cold and frosty and it is best practice not even to walk on it. In good years you may be able to mow but this would never want to be more than once during the month. Remember to avoid areas that may have spring bulbs growing in them for by the New Year they will be poking their noses above ground.

Borders

If all has gone to plan, you should have completed the tidying, leaf clearing and weeding of the borders by Christmas but this can continue if the soil isn't waterlogged or frozen. In most years, planting can also continue into December; after then the ground is normally too cold for the plants to establish well and you will be better to delay until early spring.

Early winter is a good time to empty the compost and leaf mould heaps, spreading the contents on the still warm soil. Avoid covering the crowns of the plants although some of the less hardy plants can benefit from the extra protection from cold that this can provide.

Bulbs

The earliest of the spring bulbs – the winter aconites and snowdrops – can begin to flower soon after Christmas, reaching their peak towards the end of January and into February. In milder areas daffodils start flowering in January too, although most places will have to wait another four to six weeks before they commence. Take notes or photographs of those areas that require more to be planted for it is very difficult to remember at planting time in September what is required.

If you have grown bulbs in pots for the house, or been given them as presents, stand them outside in a sheltered spot when they have finished blooming to be planted into the ground as soon as conditions permit.

Trees and shrubs

Check any ties and supports during the winter and loosen these if they are becoming too tight. Many trees are disfigured and occasionally even killed by ties that are left on too long, literally cutting the branch or trunk in half as the plant grows. At the same time, check those that have been recently planted for wind rock and firm the soil and improve support where necessary.

The cold days of January and February are the months to carry out pruning of many deciduous trees, especially if these are decoratively trained. It is essential that this is completed before the sap begins to rise, pumping new life into them as they awaken for spring, which starts to happen long before there are any outward signs of the new season.

Fruit trees and bushes such as red and blackcurrants and gooseberries can also be pruned now, as can the majority of summer-flowering ornamental shrubs.

Check plant ties periodically and don't allow them to get too tight

If the ground isn't frozen or waterlogged, trees, shrubs and new hedges can be planted and it is often possible to buy these bare-rooted, i.e. without soil, during their dormant season, a very cost effective method of purchasing.

Some vigorous climbers can become out of control and it is better to cut them back now rather than to leave them until they have become such a nuisance that the whole plant has to be removed altogether, even if that risks losing a year's flowering.

Wisterias send out huge volumes of growth each year, their wiry stems growing several feet each summer, and it is easy to be intimidated by the sight of huge numbers of tangled stems extending in all directions. Left out of control, they choke gutters, lift roof tiles and can completely cover windows, yet there is no finer sight than a well maintained specimen in full flower. Ideally, wisterias are pruned in the summer with another, major pruning session taking place during the winter. If you have not had the time to attend to the summer prune it is essential that you carry out this task. Those lengths that you need to keep to extend the size of the plant, should be tied in place now; the others should be cut to within two buds of the main stem that they have grown from. Apart from giving you a climber that is controllable once again, the pruning stimulates the production of flower buds.

If your climber is a tangled mass of dead and living stems don't be daunted. Cut back most of this growth roughly to where you want the plant to be, avoiding severing the thickest stems, and clear away. You should now be able to see the branches you want to keep so now proceed with more care to achieve the result you want.

Large-flowered clematis can be cut back to 30cm of the ground now.

Winter is the ideal time for checking and replacing ties and supports as most climbers will have lost their leaves. New wires should be fitted horizontally about 30cm apart and both they and their fittings should be strong enough to support the mature climber which can be surprisingly heavy. New growth should be loosely tied to the wires and not allowed to grow behind which often results in their being damaged.

The upper window and gutter of this house have been smothered by creepers. Climbers should always enhance a property

CHAPTER SEVEN

How to Control Pests, Diseases and Weeds

It is always disappointing when plants look poorly or die despite every endeavour to grow them well. One that has looked healthy can change suddenly, its leaves yellowing or becoming marked or eaten. Sometimes the plant can seem to have disappeared overnight; others deteriorate slowly over a much longer period. How do you recognise the symptoms or go about treating them? Even better, how do you prevent this from happening?

The sooner you react to plants that are failing through pests or disease the more likely you are to be able to save the plant.

Organic or non-organic – how to decide

If you have strong views about conservation and global issues you will probably have already decided that growing organically is for you. Others may have no qualms about the use of chemicals in the garden and choose to reach for sprays at the first sign of trouble.

As always, there is a middle way and you may feel more comfortable with using chemicals in some areas of control and preferring to follow organic principles in others. As with every other aspect of gardening there are few rigid rules and it is important to work out a regime that you feel comfortable with.

Using chemicals is often the speedier option but should never be your only consideration as many pests and diseases can be prevented by good gardening practice or by the use of physical barriers. Chemicals may eradicate your problem in the short term but it may have also killed off the many beneficial predators and organisms which will, in turn, aggravate the problem. As more and more regulations come into force restricting their use, or banning them altogether, a number of controls are being removed from the market leaving organic methods your only option.

Garden chemicals can be divided into two groups – systemic, which remain within or on the plant or the ground for a period of time, or contact, which only affect the pest or disease upon contact and leaves no residue. These often have to be used a number of times in a season as the problem re-emerges. With all chemicals, it is essential to use the right product and details for their use are always given on their packaging.

Always carefully follow the instructions when using garden chemicals. If you don't you may harm the plant, the environment and, perhaps even more important, yourself.

Regardless of which method you decide to use, good hygiene and work practice will always be beneficial.

Not all is necessarily lost if a plant does become infected but do be ruthless when it comes to removing those parts that are badly diseased or contaminated. Always burn them or put them into the municipal recycling bins as home composting may not kill off the problem. Occasionally it is more sensible to destroy the whole plant rather than risk cross contamination but look upon this as an opportunity to plant something new rather than as a failure.

Recognising pests and what to do about them

Just as you will never have a completely weed-free garden neither will you have one that does not have any pests in it. Organic gardeners are far more likely to accept a certain degree of damage to their plants than non-organic ones. If you use chemical sprays you should always think twice before reaching for the chemical bottle, for the sake of the planet as well as your purse, and all alternative options should be considered first.

Not all creepy-crawlies that you find on your plants are damaging them and many will be feeding off pest species. If you have gone down the organic route nature will in time balance itself but it may be necessary to make some hard decisions about what sorts of plants you grow in your garden. Some

Soapy water and patience is all that is needed to clear this plant of sooty mould

plants are far more susceptible to pest attack than others.

Unfortunately, some birds and animals also damage our gardens and even hardened pest controllers may baulk at the idea of harming these. It is possible, in many cases, to deter them but some can be remarkably persistent.

Insects – friend or foe?

Predators need to move fast to catch their prey and although this isn't a foolproof guide, if something is speeding along the ground or over your plants it will probably be doing much more good than harm. It is the slow-moving ones that munch their way along, or the static ones that drink the sap of your plants, that are likely to be causing problems. However, most plants can cope with some damage; it is when the pest numbers build up that it becomes unacceptable. Experience will tell you when this is the case.

Quite often it is the damage caused, rather than the pest itself, that is first noticed and it is from these signs that a decision will have to be made as to the course of treatment. There are no hard and fast rules about when pest levels rise to an unacceptable level; it all depends on whether you are prepared to accept the consequences or not. Some plants are much more susceptible to pest and disease attack than others and if you do not want to control them you may want to reconsider having that particular type of plant in your garden. Roses, for example, are prone to many different sorts and may require regular treatment to keep their foliage looking healthy. If this isn't for you but you don't want to exclude them altogether, consider growing the vigorous climbing varieties through trees where you can enjoy their prolific bloom whilst their foliage is hidden from view.

Pests also live in the soil feeding on roots and if you have a plant that suddenly wilts and dies it is worth checking it carefully when you dig it up – brown or white grubs are often the culprits although slugs may also be present.

The larger pests

Not all the creatures that eat or damage your plants are tiny. In country gardens there are numerous animals that will attack them – rabbits, hare, straying sheep and cattle and deer, although the diminutive Muntjac deer, and also badgers, are now becoming pests of urban gardens too. Moles rarely damage plants although they can dislodge them; it is when they burrow beneath lawns that the problem occurs – their molehills. Squirrels, mice and voles as well as pigeons and crows can be found everywhere.

- **Mice and voles** – Mice can devour large quantities of newly planted small bulbs – they especially like crocus – whereas voles, which are slightly larger, seem to enjoy nibbling at emerging shoots in early spring, when food sources are short. The only successful way of controlling them is by trapping or poisoning. If you do the latter, ensure that any dead bodies are disposed of before they can be eaten by other wildlife or domestic cats. Vole populations can build up to huge numbers every few years before their population crashes once again so you may decide just to leave it for nature to take its course.

- **Squirrels** – The grey squirrel was introduced from North America many years ago and has become a widespread pest, damaging trees and digging up bulbs to eat.

  Bark stripping of trees, which can result in the death of a limb or even of the whole tree in severe cases, is impossible to prevent other than by eradicating the squirrels, which may require the services of a qualified pest controller. It should be remembered that under current legislation it is illegal to trap squirrels and then release them back into the wild.

An upturned, wire hanging basket placed over newly planted bulbs often deters squirrels from digging them up. They can frequently be bought very cheaply at car boot sales or markets.

• **Rabbits and hares** – Rabbits will eat many different plants and can cause endless damage and frustration. Hares, which tend to be far less frequently encountered, mostly damage young trees by nibbling at their bark. Control is an option although often the only permanent one is to fence them out. They can jump to quite a height and also burrow beneath fencing so it is important that it is installed correctly, which can be costly in even moderate sized gardens. An alternative is to protect individual plants or beds; trees can be protected with plastic or wire guards specially designed for the purpose.

   Rabbits are inquisitive animals and will often taste or scratch around new plants only to leave them alone once they are more established. They also tend to avoid strongly scented foliage such as lavender, rosemary and sage but they can be fickle and what is untouched in one garden may be ravaged in another.

• **Deer** – There are several species of deer in Britain and their numbers are increasing rapidly, making damage in gardens a more frequent occurrence. The presence of the larger species – red, fallow, sika and roe – is usually well known in an area but they are shy animals and can be deterred relatively easily although one night-time raid on a garden can be devastating. The only sure way to keep them out is fencing which will have to be at least 1.5m or more tall.

   Muntjac, introduced from Asia, is a much smaller species and quite different in appearance, often being mistaken for a greyhound or even a pig. They often live in large gardens, urban parks and wasteland, pushing their way through or under fencing to feed on flowering stems. If muntjac are visiting your garden, a regular inspection of fencing will need to be carried out as they will take advantage of any weak spots to enter.

- **Badgers** – Increasingly common and becoming more frequent in quiet, edge of town gardens, badgers rarely do much damage to a garden. However, they have been known to dig up lawns, with devastating consequences – this is usually to search for grubs if they are present. A protected species, fencing is the only practical way to keep them out although this has to be very substantial to deter them. If badgers do visit your garden regularly, it may be better just to admit defeat and enjoy their presence.

- **Moles** – The first sign of moles in the garden is always molehills appearing on lawns, created by the excavated soil from their tunnelling below the surface. If these are left they kill off the grass below and if just flattened by mowing they create the perfect seedbed, allowing weeds such as dandelion and plantain to become established. It is always well worth the effort to brush the heaps so that the soil disappears back amongst the grass blades, only possible in dry weather, or to use a leaf blower to blow them back into the grass.

The finely worked soil from molehills can make a great addition to potting composts.

Moles can be trapped if their numbers become unacceptable although there is some skill in doing so and, sometimes, more damage is caused by setting the traps than by the moles themselves. If this is the case, it may be sensible to use the services of a pest controller.

- **Dogs and cats** – Cats are usually more of an irritation in the garden with their scratching but rarely do any serious harm. If they insist upon using your seedbeds as a lavatory, protect with wire or plastic mesh.

    Dogs can cause more harm to the garden but as it is unlikely that you would choose to get rid of your pet, alternative controls have to be found. Damage from digging and urinating on lawns or plants can only really be stopped by rigorous training. This can be done quite easily but requires perseverance: try designating a specific area for these activities and reward when they are used.

    Circular, dead patches on lawns, often surrounded by lusher growth are usually caused by bitches urinating; dead, brown foliage at the base of plants, especially evergreens, is usually caused by male dogs. On frequently marked plants there is often a strong smell of urine present too.

If you don't want to banish your dog from the garden consider fencing off certain parts, for example, the vegetable or herb garden for it is unlikely you will want to have contaminated edible plants. This barrier need not be utilitarian – it can be quite decorative – but remember that even quite large dogs can push through gaps at the base of hedging and won't necessarily be deterred by thorns.

- **Birds** – Relatively little damage is caused in the decorative garden by birds. Occasionally they may peck at flowers or strip buds off ornamental trees in cold weather but the pleasure that their presence gives us and the vast numbers of pests that they consume outweighs any problems they cause.

  In the vegetable and fruit garden it is, however, different. Flocks of pigeons may descend to devour members of the cabbage tribe, blackbirds and thrushes will eat your ripening raspberries and strawberries and crows seem especially fond of eating the new shoots of broad beans – the only sure prevention is to use a netting barrier. Many other deterrents are on the market, although your unwanted CDs hanging on threads so that they glitter as they move in a breeze work to an extent but only if they are repositioned periodically. Seeds sown directly into the ground can also be targeted but damage in those places is most likely to occur by birds having dust baths in the fine, dry soil: again a temporary netting barrier is the easiest method of prevention.

Fungal diseases

Although toadstools growing around or close to a plant may indeed be a cause for concern, the majority of fungal attacks on plants are by very tiny or microscopic organisms. In many cases they remain unseen until the plant, or part of it, collapses and dies. Little can be done other than to clear and burn, or place in your municipal bin, anything that you think might have been affected in this way. Your home compost heap is unlikely to heat up enough to kill the infection.

There are some fungicides that can be used as a preventative treatment but it is impossible to protect all plants from possible infection for the spores that are the fungi's equivalent to other plants' seeds float unseen in the air in their millions, waiting to land on the correct host plant. Maintaining a tidy garden by removing fallen leaves and dead or dying plant material is probably your best general defence although, of course, you are also removing a valuable food source and shelter for beneficial wildlife. As with everything else in life, you have to compromise and lack of time or inclination will mean that you will need to focus on disposing of just those that look suspect.

The fungal diseases of leaves manifest themselves mostly as leaf spots, rusts and moulds, all looking pretty much as their names suggest. Treatment depends on just how unacceptable and practical it is – for example, blackspot, the curse of roses, which in severe cases can lead to defoliation, is treatable by spraying (although you are never likely to banish it completely). A similar leaf spot that is equally common on sycamore trees is not – not just

There is no cure for the devestating disease box blight

due to their size; it also does not appear to affect the tree that much.

The woody branches and trunks of trees and shrubs can also be attacked and often the problem can be resolved by pruning out infected and dead wood on a regular basis (see page 162). Golden brown toadstools growing at the plant's base may be those of honey fungus which will result in its death, but equally they may be of a more harmless species. Removing the toadstools will have no effect as the damage will have already been done.

There are a number of newly introduced, aggressive diseases that are affecting trees and shrubs. They are usually caused by fungal spores or insects and with no chemicals or predators to control them rapidly spread. One that can have a devastating effect in formal gardens is box blight which infects members of the *Buxus* family. It is most troublesome where box is clipped regularly such as hedges and topiary; there is no cure. The disease first shows as yellow or orange colouring of the leaves before they fall, leaving bare patches. Box leaves often turn these colours for a number of other reasons too, such as drought, starvation and waterlogging, so don't panic initially when seeing these symptoms – it will soon become clear if it is blight. With topiary there may be no option other than to remove and burn, but with hedges a number of treatments can be tried – although none have been proven to work. Try cutting the box to within 15cm of the ground, clearing and burning all leaves and wood. In many cases the plants will regrow but they may become reinfected.

It is best to cut box, whether infected or not, when rain is not forecast for several days as the blight spores are transferred by water splash. If the plants are dry, there is a better chance that the wounds may have sealed over making it more difficult for the disease to take hold.

Lawns also have their share of fungal disease, many of which can be controlled by good gardening practice such as the removal of 'thatch' by scarifying and aerating. A lot of lawn problems are exacerbated by mowing the grass too short.

How to identify common problems

Despite the huge number of potential problems that plants face from pests and diseases, the majority grow perfectly well and with few problems. Table 5 will help you identify the likely cause of some of the more common ones. The Royal Horticultural Society (RHS) website gives the latest information on controls and will also help with further diagnosis.

dandelion and plantain, both of which form ground-hugging rosettes, are quite easy to cut out manually in smaller areas or can be individually treated with weed killer. Other weeds can become invasive in turf and spraying the whole lawn with chemicals may be the only option. This can be carried out just occasionally if you don't want to do this on a regular basis, although the end result will not be as good. Remember that it is essential to use a weed killer that is specifically described for use on lawns or you may end up killing the grass as well.

Weeds in gravel and other hard surfaces

Gravel is often described as low maintenance whether used on driveways and paths or in 'gravel gardens' where decorative plants are grown directly into the soil beneath a gravel covering. It will still need some attention, however.

Gravel will require frequent weed control, although this is often easier and quicker than weeding other areas.

Chemical sprays are quick to use on wide open areas but difficult amongst plants and if you have a gravel garden it will require regular hand weeding. In dry weather, the use of a hoe is a speedy alternative to this or even to spraying quite large expanses. If hand-pulling weeds is your only

Gravel needs to be kept weed free if it is to look good

option you will find them easier to remove than when they are growing in bare soil.

Gravel does not just make an ideal seed bed for weeds to flourish, many garden plants do so too, especially lavender if one is growing nearby. If these are removed when still small they can be replanted elsewhere in the garden, although in many cases they may not be an identical match to the parent plant.

Driveways, paths, patios and terraces should always be kept weed free if your garden is to look good for here, there are no other plants to disguise them. The cracks between paving slabs are best treated with a weed killer designed for the purpose although there are special thin-bladed hand tools that can be used if going down the organic route – it is a tedious and time-consuming task however.

Weeds in the garden borders

The easiest way to control weeds is to cover the soil with plants that you really want. If you have carried out the thorough weeding as recommended in spring and autumn the majority of problems will have been resolved then, but there will always be some that have been missed and new ones appear.

As with gravel, using a hoe is a quick and satisfying method of manually controlling weeds; when used correctly it can help prevent back problems. A hoe, however, will not work well in damp conditions as many of the weeds will re-root themselves. In warmer weather they quickly shrivel and die and, if still small, disappear so do not even require removal from the soil surface.

When a hoe cannot be used, a garden fork may be your only option and a lightweight and small border fork is best for this. The technique here is not to dig too deeply but to loosen the soil releasing the weeds so that they can be pulled out by hand as you go along.

Although relying on a complete list of weeds is not practical or even desirable – for you will soon learn through practice what should or should not be growing – there are a few weeds that do need special mention. This is because they can be so difficult to control and all too easy to spread to other parts of the garden even when you are fully aware of the problem.

Ground elder and bindweed, both rampant weeds, have a bright white running root system which is an easy way of identifying them below ground.

- **Bindweed** – *Calystegia sepium* – A very common and troublesome weed that sends out long, thin, twining stems that wrap tightly around plants to a height of 3m or more. If left it can smother plants, fences and hedges before single, white trumpet-like flowers appear. Its roots can go 4.5m or more into the ground, making it impossible to remove all of these; where sections are dug out any part that breaks off can regrow to create a new plant. Although bindweed is persistent, it will weaken over time and can be eradicated with perseverance.

  Where other plants are growing, weed killer cannot be used as it will kill any plant it touches. This makes it very difficult to use in the majority of places so instead dig as much of the root out as possible with a fork. If this isn't feasible because of other plants that want to be kept, hoe or pull the plant. Don't be tempted just to pull the twining stems from the host plant as you are likely to remove the host's leaves and flowers as well. The simplest method is to sever the stems at ground level and leave them for a while – even an hour will do – the bindweed will have relaxed its grip and come away far more readily. Without doing this it is a much more difficult and time-consuming task to untangle them. Occasionally you

Despite the beauty of its flower, bindweed is an unwelcome and difficult weed to control in the garden

will come across methods of control that suggest getting the bindweed to grow up bamboo canes so that you isolate them from other plants – this wastes precious time organising when you could be doing other things and rarely seems to work that well.

There is a smaller version of bindweed with pale pink flowers (*Convolvulus arvensis*) which has just as troublesome a root system although it is less frequently encountered in gardens.

Place all parts of bindweed in the municipal bins for disposal or burn.

- **Couch grass** – *Elymus repens* – Sometimes known as twitch, this grass looks just like any other above ground but when dug has a network of thin white 'roots' (stolons) travelling in all directions. These are extremely brittle and break readily, regrowing from each piece. They are difficult to eradicate other than by careful hand weeding out as they quickly spread into the root systems of other plants. Where this happens with smaller plants such as herbaceous, it may become necessary to dig them up and carefully tease out the couch or discard the desired plant altogether. If couch is growing beneath shrubs or fruit bushes it may be possible to spray the couch with a weed killer containing glyphosate, providing you are able to prevent it from touching any greenery other than the grass.

  Couch grass in lawns tends to be less troublesome as it does not cope well with being mown, but its root systems may invade adjacent borders. There are no weed killers for lawns that will only kill couch grass and leave the other lawn grasses untouched.

  Dispose of dug out couch grass in the same way as bindweed – do not place it in your compost heap.

- **Ground elder** – *Aegopodium podagraria* – A common weed in older, established gardens and another troublesome one to eradicate. An herbaceous plant, it disappears in the winter to send out new bright green leaves in early spring. Rapid growth will create dense carpets of leaves up to 15cm high, with taller stems topped by flat heads of tiny white flowers throughout summer. Only the most robust of garden plants can cope with these infestations and chemical control is difficult if desired plants are not to be destroyed.

  Ground elder rarely seeds but spreads by a white root system which readily breaks to create new plants. These remain close to the surface so careful cultivation can reduce the problem; once amongst other plants, controls similar to couch grass may be your only option.

When weeding out ground elder it is worthwhile carefully following the root system along the ground with a small fork, pulling gently as you go. Often what appears to be a small leaf on the surface will have a root that has travelled several feet and it is sometimes possible to get a large amount of this out in one go. Continual weeding will reduce the problem to manageable levels although it is unlikely to be eradicated altogether. It is possible to buy from garden centres glyphosate in gel form and hand paint the weed killer onto the ground elder's leaves. This is very time consuming and only viable in very small areas but may be worth trying if a precious plant has become infested.

There is a form of ground elder with variegated leaves that is occasionally offered for sale as an ornamental plant. If you are tempted to try it ensure that it is grown in pots or in areas where there is no risk of it spreading too much as it is just as invasive as its plain green-leafed version.

Ground elder can sometimes be present in grass but rarely persists if mown regularly.

Ground elder leaves – but not the roots – can be put in the compost heap but it is probably easier and wiser to burn or place in council bins.

- **Horsetail –** *Equisetum arvense* **–** When you discover horsetail has been found in fossil records and survived the Ice Age it makes you realise that it is going to take a lot of effort on your part to eradicate it. Fortunately, it is not commonly found in gardens although it may be brought in unwittingly through contaminated garden soil or even as an attractive purchase at a garden fete.

  Stiff, brittle, dark green bottlebrushes make horsetail instantly recognisable. It has a brown cord-like root system which makes the pieces that readily break off very difficult to see. If you have horsetail in the border, pulling may be the only way to control it and this will need to be carried out regularly. In grass, constant mowing is effective. Neither will eradicate it but will help to hide it.

  Chemical controls can only be used where no other plants are growing and it may take a number of years of regular treatment before it is fully eradicated making this, in the majority of cases, an unrealistic approach.

- **Japanese knotweed – *Fallopia japonica*** Growing to 2m tall or more in a single season, this perennial plant was introduced into gardens by the Victorians. Treatment is very difficult for the roots penetrate the soil to a great depth making digging out impossible. Every part of the plant will root where it falls and can easily be transported to other parts of the garden on clothing or footwear so even cutting down the stems can prove risky. If you should attempt this it is important to leave the stems where they are to dry out before burning on site. Classified as controlled waste under environmental protection laws you should not place any part of it in bins for disposal.

  Fortunately, Japanese knotweed is not commonly encountered. Its attractive, tall, purple-blotched stems and large, pale green leaves are occasionally found in old gardens or introduced from plants growing in the wild. It is possible that a biological control in the form of a sap-sucking insect may become available to gardeners within the next few years once assessment trials have been completed.

- **Ragwort – *Senecio jacobaea* –** This is another species introduced as a garden ornamental which has now spread into fields and roadside verges. It occasionally appears in gardens as a grey-green basal rosette of deeply cut leaves before sending up a 60cm flower spike topped with numerous bright yellow daisy flowers. Although attractive, the plant should be removed as it seeds prolifically and when grazed by livestock is very poisonous.

  Dig the plant out by its roots and watch for further regrowth or new self-sown ones appearing. Every part of the plant is toxic and if you should have a paddock or large numbers of the plants growing great care is needed in handling. It is important to wear gloves, especially if pulling the plant, as the sap from the bruised stems and leaves is absorbed through the skin.

  Place all parts of the plant in your municipal bin or burn.

CHAPTER EIGHT

Pruning Without Fear

It goes without saying that if you want your garden to look its best at all times then you need to keep your plants in the best condition. This does not just mean worrying about pest and disease attack – many are lost through lack of pruning. When we talk about 'pruning', the term refers to the cutting back of plants that have woody stems and/or branches, i.e. mostly trees and shrubs. Herbaceous plants are not usually included in this term for although they are also cut back at times such as the end of the season nearly all of them require the same simple treatment. Trees and shrubs, because they continue to grow for many years, are more exacting in their requirements and it is this that gives the impression that it is complicated work. It does not have to be so.

What happens when a tree or a shrub is allowed to grow unchecked over many years? Apart from getting larger some improve as their natural shape and stature are attained. They continue to look healthy and flower or fruit well and may even be the major part of the 'wow' factor that we are striving for – if that is the case, leave well alone. However, quite often it is different. They still get larger but they outgrow their allotted space, perhaps obstructing paths or light and creating an imbalance in the garden's appearance. More and more dead branches build up within the plant (this happens especially with some climbers) and sometimes flowering and fruiting dwindles. In desperation the whole plant is chopped down and removed. Regular pruning will prevent this and, if you haven't got around to it or have just inherited a plant like this, a more severe restoration treatment may rejuvenate it.

If you have a tree, shrub or climber that has greatly outgrown its space it may still be saveable. Consider pruning it severely before removing it altogether – the technique is really quite simple.

Five simple rules for easier pruning

Rule 1: 'Have courage' – Many gardeners, whether experienced or not, are timid when it comes to pruning. If this sounds like you, this is your most important rule which can loosely be interpreted as 'cut as much away as you dare and then cut half as much again'.

Rule 2: The rule of the three Ds – Dead, Diseased or Damaged: cut away any branches that fit into this category, which can be sometimes, rather alarmingly, most of a plant. Many plants regrow quite healthily after drastic treatment but you will have to decide if you want to persevere with one that is badly disfigured. If it ends up very misshapen or ugly then it is probably best to remove it. Remember that there is no such thing as a dead disaster in gardening – just an opportunity to plant something new.

Rule 3: Prune evergreens in summer – Avoid pruning between the end of August and the end of April for frosts or cold winds can damage the tender, new growth that appears after pruning.

Rule 4: Don't be in a rush – You should spend as much time looking at the plant considering where to make the cuts as you do in actually carrying out the work. Try to visualise the shape that you would like the plant to end up as and prune accordingly – after every few cuts, stand back and review progress.

Rule 5: Use the right tools for the job – It sounds obvious but all too frequently damage is caused to plants by using inappropriate tools. This is discussed in detail on page 181.

Knowing when to prune

If you have a plant that is obstructing a path or blocking out light from a window then you need to prune it regardless of what time of year it is unless, of course, you feel able to live with the problem for a while. For every other reason then, ideally, the time to prune depends on the type of tree or shrub it is. This can lead to some confusion but there are some simple guidelines that help to clarify the issue. Table 6 shows the pruning times for shrubs.

Trees can be treated similarly – just look upon them as large shrubs on sticks. However it is best to leave any but the smallest of trees to the professionals, both for the sake of safety and for the tree itself. Mature fruit trees – apples, pears, plums and cherries – are often found in established gardens, or new ones being planted, and these are pruned rather differently to other types and the pruning of these are detailed separately.

Table 6: Shrub pruning

	When to prune	Examples
Shrubs that flower in spring or early summer	Immediately after flowering	Forsythia Ribes (flowering currants) Deutzia
Shrubs that flower from midsummer onwards	Early spring	Buddleia Perovskia Spiraea
Evergreens	May – August	Box (*Buxus*) Rosemary
Shrubs with silvery leaves Lavender	April April and/or August	Cotton lavender (*Santolina*)

Pruning spring-flowering shrubs

Shrubs and hedges are used by wild birds both for breeding, shelter and feeding. Make sure before you start pruning that you are not disturbing nests or depriving them of food, such as berries in winter.

Making the pruning cut

Pruning is quite an easy task but it is important that the cuts are made in the correct way for you want to minimise the risk of disease entry and improve the appearance of the plant. Messy pruning may not kill off a shrub but it will make it look, well, just messy.

Take a close look at different plants in your garden and see how the leaves grow away from the stems. If it is winter and there are no leaves, the leaf bud will still be visible; in summer both buds and leaves can be seen. In some plants pairs of leaves and buds are found to be opposite one another; in other species, single leaves can be found growing on alternate sides of the stem.

When a branch is cut, the buds immediately below the cut are stimulated to create a replacement branch and they grow roughly at the angle that the bud is pointing. As it is never desirable to have branches growing inwards, the secret is always to prune to an outer bud pointing in the direction that you want it to grow in.

The actual cut itself should be made quite close to the bud – too close and you may damage it, too far away and you leave a stub of branch that will die back and look unsightly. Check the following illustration – you will see that the alternate buds are cut at the same angle as the bud is growing; the opposite buds are cut straight.

Angle of pruning cut for alternate leaf (or bud)

Angle of pruning cut for opposite leaf (or bud)

What to do if you don't know what sort of shrub it is

However experienced a gardener you are or may become, you will inevitably come across plants that you don't recognise. How can you decide how to prune it if you cannot look it up in a garden manual? The answer is to look thoroughly inside the shrub for clues, not always easy if the plant is a dense thicket of stems (although that is a clue in itself).

When you peer into a shrub you are looking to see how the plant is growing. If there are leaves and signs of new growth coming from ground level or close to it, especially if they are growing out of stems that have obviously been there for a few years, you can be quite confident that you are able to prune as low as you wish.

Likewise, if when you look there are none of these signs and all the new growth is happening at the top of the shrub, you may need to prune much less severely. Sometimes the signs are midway and, again, you prune accordingly.

Occasionally, the answers are still not clear and the trick on these occasions – assuming you

New growth coming from old, thick stems hint that this shrub can be pruned as hard as you like

have the time to wait – is to prune some stems at all three levels and see where the new growth appears. Pruning at three levels is a good way to extend the flowering period of some plants as, depending on the species, the older growth flowers first to be followed on by the more severely pruned stems. The large-flowered clematis responds especially well to this treatment.

Remember that it isn't always necessary to prune. Only do so if you want to improve or restrict the shape and size or to remove dead, damaged or diseased branches. Pruning sometimes will improve flowering and fruiting too.

How to prune fruit trees

Although the basic principles for pruning fruit trees are really no different to any other tree or shrub, as you are aiming to achieve maximum cropping it is important to consider this when pruning. This has led to a lot of mystery surrounding it but, as always, there are some simple methods that work well. Apart from controlling the size of the tree, pruning acts as a stimulus, converting leaf buds to ones that will bear fruit.

Apples and pears

If you are worried about losing fruit through incorrect pruning you will find it very much easier if you carry this out in midsummer for the blossom or young fruit will be visible. The correct time for this summer pruning is when the very last leaf has opened fully – this is always the one at the very tip of the tree and it usually opens much later than all the rest. Some years this will happen earlier or later than others; it makes no difference what the date is for it is another example of your working 'with the season'.

Summer pruning reduces the amount of new shoots that the tree will send out which is ideal if you are trying to restrict its size.

If you require the tree to put on an additional spurt of growth or have been just too busy or forgotten to prune in summer, then carry out the pruning when the tree is dormant in midwinter, January or February being ideal if there aren't exceptionally heavy frosts at night.

When you look at your fruit tree you will see that at the tips of the branches there are long-growing shoots with no side shoots. If you do not want these branches to continue to grow and enlarge the tree, then prune them back to about four buds or approximately half their length. All the time remember that you are trying to achieve a tree that looks well balanced so some branches may need to be pruned more than others.

You may come across trees that haven't been allowed to develop naturally but have been trained to grow against walls, either by having a central trunk with 'arms' stretching out horizontally (espaliers) or where the trees have been planted on the slant (cordons) with side branching severely restricted. Occasionally these are planted as free-standing 'dividers', trained along wires and separating different parts of the garden and they are most attractive when used in this way. With both of these growth forms the secret is to prune back any shoots that face either inwards or outwards, the remaining shoots being pruned as normal. As always, doing it is easier than reading about it so don't be too anxious about 'having a go' – after all, the very worst that can happen is that you may end up with a reduced crop of fruit that year.

Cherries and plums

Because fungal disease is rife with cherries and plums it is important to prune them as little as possible. If you carry out a regular pruning regime when the trees are still young the branches and, therefore, the wounds are small but often you inherit a tree that has been allowed to grow unchecked. In either case, prune in July and August when they are less susceptible to attack.

Even relatively young plum trees can fruit heavily and, if this should happen, it is a wise precaution to support their branches with props as they may snap under the weight. If this has happened make a clean cut with a pruning saw as soon as you notice it to reduce the amount of open wound for disease to enter.

Sometimes, in spring, you will find lengths of new growth that are showing no signs of leaf or blossom at all. Invariably, birds – especially bullfinches – have eaten the buds during the winter months. These stripped branches should be pruned back to a healthy bud as soon as it becomes obvious, usually around March.

How to prune roses

The pruning of roses is another mystery to many gardeners but, again, it is straightforward if you remember certain principles. One to bear in mind is that roses come in a wide range of sizes so some are always going to be larger than others. Another is to try and keep the centre, if it is a non-climbing type, fairly 'open'. This means removing many of the central branches so that air can circulate freely amongst them which, in turn, reduces the prevalence of some diseases. Treat rose trees in the same way for they are simply bush roses atop a tall, single stem; any shoots coming from ground level or along this stem should be completely removed.

It is not realistic to keep a rose that wants to grow to 2m tall in all directions at half a metre and still expect it to flower well.

Climbing roses can also be pruned although there is very little point in trying to do this to a 9m rambling rose scrambling through a tall tree – a beautiful way, incidentally, of growing roses with very little effort. Some climbers produce long, flexible stems from the base of the plant – cut the old stems to ground level as soon after flowering as possible and tie in the new growths which will flower the following summer. Tie the stems in to create a fan shape, for the more horizontal the stem, the greater the flowering. Others don't send out shoots from the base, instead these appear further up the plant. These are treated differently although, ideally, they should be tied in place close to horizontal as they grow. During late autumn to early spring the old flowering shoots, which appear as short spurs off the main branches, should be pruned back to three or four leaf buds.

All roses grow with alternate leaves so the pruning cut is always at the diagonal.

How to maintain a natural shape

All too often after shrubs have been pruned they look an odd shape and unattractive. One of the most common errors is to reduce all their branches to the same height which gives them a stubby appearance. Occasionally this is necessary, for example, when they are planted immediately beneath a window. Visually, most shrubs benefit from being pruned so that they look like a scaled down version of their original size or are able to grow naturally back into it.

Pruning climbers

Take great care when stems and tendrils have become wrapped around telephone or electrical cables. It is essential that these are disentangled and pruned out but it can be remarkably hard to distinguish which is which. Frequently, it has been forgotten that cables are running behind a long planted climber and it is irritating at the very least if these are damaged.

Many climbers will not require any regular pruning and can be left quite happily for many years. There are a few, however, that benefit from attention:

• **Clematis** – Pruning guides can be over complicated for the majority respond quite well to two different regimes. The rampant spring or early summer flowering varieties – the montanas, alpinas and macropetalas – are easiest if they are clipped with hedging shears immediately after flowering to control their growth. However, *clematis montana* is still likely to get out of hand and it may be necessary to prune it hard every few years to near ground level and allow it to regrow. One of the best ways of growing it is to allow it to scramble up a tall tree where you will have all the benefits of their free flowering without the effort of pruning.

The evergreen clematis, *Clematis armandii* (which is often sold under the variety name 'Apple Blossom'), flowers in early spring and grows best when given the shelter of a warm, south or west-facing wall. In this situation it can become quite vigorous, growing to 7.5m or more and flowering high above eye level. It doesn't always respond well to pruning and often stems that you have carefully moved to tie into place die back for no obvious reason. Sometimes you just have to take the chance with an out-of-control specimen and deal with it by pruning as you would the other spring-flowering clematis.

Clematis that have larger flowers during the summer are the easiest of all – simply cut down to 30cm above ground level, or their lowest pair of buds, during the winter. This pruning regime makes them ideal for growing through shrubs and other plants as an otherwise untidy appearance is removed. What happens if you don't prune? The plants will still flower but ever higher with bare or dead stems at eye level. These dead stems often build up so that the whole plant becomes a tangled and unat-tractive mess – pruning hard avoids this. An alternative method of pruning is to cut the stems at three different heights. The advantage of this is that the clematis will flower over a longer period of time and to a greater height.

Check all climbers periodically to ensure that they aren't choking gutters or smothering lesser plants.

- **Honeysuckle** – *Lonicera* – When growing through trees or in an out of the way spot it probably isn't necessary or practical to prune it at all, although it can be pruned as severely as clematis if rejuvenation is required. Those growing against walls or in places where they need to be controlled can have their side branches cut back to two pairs of buds immediately after flowering. Do this, too, if their leaves get covered in a white powdery mould which often happens when grown in dry situations

- **Hydrangea** – Climbing hydrangeas are useful and attractive, self-clinging shrubs for planting against a shady, north wall. They are easy to grow and require little maintenance. However, if they extend too far away from the wall their branches, which are quite brittle, can break in strong winds and so may need pruning back periodically to keep them in check. It is also essential to keep them away from gutters and downpipes and they will also quite happily attach themselves to window frames. Prune back to a pair of buds, after flowering, wherever you like. They can withstand a severe pruning back to their main trunks, if necessary – this is best carried out during the winter but, of course, there will be few flowers for the first couple of years after this treatment.

- **Ivy** – *Hedera* – Ivy is one of those climbers that you either love or loathe. Pruning can take place at any time of year and usually consists of cutting back any unwanted stems at any point. Sometimes the side branches can extend quite far out from the main ones and these can be cut severely back – using shears or even a hedge trimmer will save valuable time.

- **Jasmine** – *Jasminum* – Both summer and winter-flowering jasmines benefit from being pruned for often dead wood builds up beneath the new flowering stems. Winter jasmine can be pruned hard back close to its main stems immediately after flowering. The summer-flowering sorts can also have this treatment when they become too untidy or have an annual clipping with hedging shears immediately after they flower.

  The so-called evergreen jasmine, *Trachelospermum*, is far less vigorous and like other evergreens should be pruned in the summer months – but only if this proves necessary.

Cutting hedges

Hedges are planted to define garden boundaries or to create divisions or shelter within the garden and may vary from just a foot or so to many feet in height requiring ladders to reach their tops.

To keep them looking at their best, hedges need regular clipping although, as we are always trying to make our gardening time as productive and enjoyable as possible, we need to look at ways of minimising the hours spent on it.

A number of features could be adapted from this country garden

If you are planting a new hedge consider what the long-term aim is and if there are any ways that maintenance time could be saved. For example, yew makes a great evergreen screen but only looks at its very best if cut accurately with sharp angles and kept 'tight' by regular clipping. A traditional mixed farm hedge of hawthorn, hazel, blackthorn and other native shrubs is ideal for a country garden boundary but is more difficult to keep looking neat. Any hedging plant with thorns or spines may be a problem – they may deter intruders but they will almost certainly slow down the clearing away of the cuttings unless you wear the stoutest of leather gloves.

It is desirable to lightly trim young hedging as this encourages a dense network of branches and will give better screening than if they are left to grow unchecked; once annually is usually often enough.

Mature hedges also can be cut annually but in some species and situations you may need to trim twice or even three times a year to keep it looking neat. This can become quite a chore so consider whether the whole length of hedging needs this treatment – there may be sections further away from the house that could be just cut once. If you have a lot of hedging and hate the task then this is definitely a job that could be worth hiring someone else to do – gardening is all about enjoyment so don't burden yourself unnecessarily.

Formal hedges, such as box and yew, need to be accurately clipped and much satisfaction can be got from achieving this. Other species are often allowed to form a looser structure where such accuracy is not necessary.

As with other pruning, trim evergreen hedging during the summer months. Deciduous hedging – those that lose their leaves in the winter – are often pruned in the summer months too, but winter pruning is often preferable as you may have fewer maintenance tasks to carry out then.

Finer hedge clippings can be added to the compost heap and are a good source of 'browns' that help balance out the 'greens' of mowings and other garden waste. See page 108 for more details. Any thorny clippings are best excluded.

A number of different tools can be used for hedge cutting, ranging from hand shears to powered trimmers. Secateurs may occasionally need to be used for very accurate cutting. These are discussed in detail in Chapter 9.

- **Beech – *Fagus sylvatica* –** The advantage of beech hedging is that it is relatively quick to establish and, although deciduous, holds onto its golden-bronze, autumn-coloured leaves through the winter. These are pushed off by the unfurling new green ones in spring which does mean that you may have to carry out some leaf collecting when you least expect it. Usually, one cut annually is enough – if carried out during the winter you will lose some of the retained leaf cover.

- **Box – *Buxus sempervirens* –** Box hedging is ideally suited as a low edging around flower borders and herb gardens and is often used in this way for it takes very many years to grow to any great height. It is essential, if it is to look good, that it is clipped accurately and regularly – if necessary, put string lines stretched taut between canes to guide you or, if you prefer, cut by eye. The photos show how an out-of-shape box hedge can be transformed in a matter of hours. Box can often be given just one good clipping a year although you may need to give a second, lighter one (no later than August).

A string line may help you clip more accurately   The finished result – clean crisp lines

See page 149 for information on box blight and the precautions that can be taken to try to avoid this troublesome new disease.

- **Conifers** – The Leyland Cypress (*x Cuprocyparis leylandii*) has become synonymous with enormously tall hedging subject to neighbour disputes and court orders which is a pity for as a fast-growing, evergreen, dense hedge it has few rivals. When grown well and clipped regularly it has a fine texture. In recent years attack by cypress aphid has become more prevalent and it is often this that causes unsightly dead patches; severe cutting may also result in brown foliage. Whatever the cause, the dead patches take a very long time to be replaced by new growth and often results in the hedges being replaced.

  Other hedging conifers commonly used are the Lawson cypress, *Chamaecyparis lawsoniana*, and the western red cedar, *Thuja plicata*, both of which are treated in the same way as the Leyland and are prone to the same problems although they are not quite as fast growing.

  Hedge cutting should take place between April and August – up to three times annually for the very best finish. With newly planted conifer hedges, clip back any overlong side-shoots by half in April each year until the hedge has reached its required height, then reduce its height by up to 15–30cm to allow for regrowth.

  Overgrown hedges can be difficult to tackle and you may find it necessary to hire a tree surgeon. If you decide to tackle it yourself, cut back the sides as much as possible without exposing the inner dead brown wood. Removing the tops can be difficult and can result in an unattractive finish. Cutting them so that the uppermost branches conceal the top of the exposed trunk from ground level may help improve the hedge's appearance. With severe pruning there is always a risk that some of the plants may die.

- **Hornbeam** – *Carpinus betulus* – Similar in appearance to beech and treated in the same way, hornbeam is more tolerant of shade and heavy, clay soils. Its dense twiggy branches make it ideal for pleaching, sometimes described as 'hedges on legs'. These are treated in exactly the same way as normal hedges – it is essential that you take time to get both a level top and bottom to the hedge or they look dreadful.

- **Holly** – *Ilex aquifolium* – Holly hedges are dense and prickly and make good and attractive barriers. As with other evergreens, clip in summer. One major disadvantage is that they shed their old leaves which collect on the ground beneath them, their sharp spines making clearing painful.

- **Laurel** – *Prunus laurocerasus* – Shiny, evergreen leaves make laurel an ideal screen but they can become massive if not regularly clipped. Often garden manuals will advise pruning each stem individually to avoid damaging the large leaves but, for most people, this is not an option. Cut during the summer with shears or a hedge trimmer and take a chance – you can always hand prune any stems that look shabby.

- **Lavender** – *Lavandula angustifolia* – As a scented, low-growing edging to a path, patio or terrace, lavender has no equal. If not kept clipped, they have a tendency to become leggy and bare stemmed at the base and it is very difficult to restore them once they reach this stage. Replace with new plants and clip quite hard in August, even if it means sacrificing some of the flowers. Even with this regular treatment you may find that it is necessary to replant every few years to keep the hedging looking at its best.

- *Lonicera* – Not often planted these days but used extensively in the past, it is still found in some older gardens. Rapid growing, its branches covered with tiny, dark green (occasionally golden yellow) leaves, Lonicera is a non-flowering and non-climbing form of honeysuckle. It requires frequent clipping – sometimes three or more times a year – to look its best. If left unclipped and allowed to grow tall, Lonicera often literally topples over and you may find it sprawling on the ground. In this situation cut back all stems, young and old, to within a few inches from ground level; it will quickly regrow.

- **Privet** – *Ligustrum ovalifolium* – Privet was widely used in the past as a rapidly growing hedge before Leylandii conifers became the rage and requires clipping twice yearly to remain dense. Although described as evergreen it may drop its leaves in very cold winters, new ones regrowing in the spring.

- **Yew** – *Taxus baccata* – The aristocrat of fine hedges with dense, dark green, evergreen foliage that lends itself to the formal garden, clipped regularly and accurately it cannot be surpassed. As with all evergreens, trim during the summer months.

How to renovate an overgrown hedge

Most hedges whatever their condition, apart from conifers (yew excepted), can be brought back to shape by drastic pruning although the process will take a few years to complete.

Just because a hedge has been left to grow out of control, all is not lost. The majority of hedging plants respond to radical pruning which is much easier than replacing it.

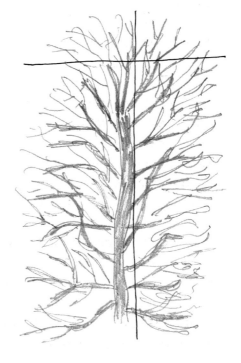

The most extreme way is to cut the whole hedge down to 15cm above ground level, preferably in winter when the plants are dormant if they are deciduous or in early summer if they are evergreen. Their extensive root system acts as a powerhouse and new growth is rapid,

Hedge regeneration

Sedum often collapses under the weight of its flower heads and is a prime candidate for the 'Chelsea Chop'

especially if you can feed them with compost or a general-purpose fertiliser. Treat the hedge as if it has been newly planted, clipping back any over long side shoots by up to half their length to encourage bushiness.

An alternative method if you don't want to lose the screening height of the hedge is to cut back just one side of it to within a few inches of the main trunks. At the same time reduce the height, by as much as 50 per cent, to about 30cm below the desired finished height. Feed the hedge and clip as described above. If regrowth has been plentiful, the following year can have the remaining side pruned back in the same way. If it has not regrown well it is advisable to leave cutting the second side for a further year.

In dry summers, water the hedge to keep it growing well.

The 'Chelsea chop'

There are a number of herbaceous plants that have a tendency to collapse just as they are about to flower. This can be avoided by staking but unless it is done before the plant flops, or with great care, it can result in a spoilt appearance. This may be one too many tasks to be added to an already over-long list at a busy time of the gardening year. An alternative is to carry out a radical but simple pruning technique called the 'Chelsea chop', so called because it is done about the same time of year as the Chelsea Flower Show – the end of May or early June.

All stems on the plant are cut back by one third or as much as half of their height using shears or secateurs. Although this delays flowering, the blooms will be more numerous, smaller and on shorter stems. Another option is to cut just part of the plant which will mean that although some may require support the flowering period will be extended.

Flowers that are suitable for this treatment include most of those with a daisy-shaped flower head, the taller Campanula, Phlox and, best of all, the fleshy leaved, taller varieties of Sedum which always collapse weighed down by the heaviness of their blooms.

If in doubt as to what you can prune, experiment by cutting just a few stems back the first year. Plants that naturally only send up a single flower spike are best left untouched.

CHAPTER NINE

What Tools Do I Really Need?

There is a huge array of garden tools available on the market and the choice can be quite confusing. Start by buying the basics, making sure that they feel comfortable and well balanced before you leave the store.

Building up a collection of tools can be quite expensive but it can be false economy to buy the cheapest. Car boot sales are often a good source of well made, used tools sold cheaply.

The list below is a guide and you may not need every item that is on it – your own list will vary depending on the size of your garden and the type of jobs you want to do.

Hand tools
Forks

If you have flower borders or grow vegetables, forks are essential. For general use, a **border fork** is good – lightweight and small enough to get amongst plants without damaging them. For digging over big areas a **standard sized fork**, larger and heavier, is more practical. **Hand forks**, which are very small, are used for working with pots and are also good for weeding edges of borders or bulb planting.

Spades

You will only need to buy a spade if you intend to dig holes for planting, although for smaller, potted plants a fork and trowel are perfectly adequate. Spades are also good digging tools, used instead of a fork, although the technique can take a little practice to master: the secret is to take small sized 'bites' of soil rather than large, heavy spadefuls that rapidly tire you out.

Spades, like forks, come in different sizes. The **border spade** is the counterpart of the border fork and there is also a **standard sized spade**. A very long handled spade with a pointed blade – sometimes called an **Irish spade** – is good for digging large areas as you work in an upright position which helps against back strain.

Trowels

These little hand tools are indispensable for planting out smaller plants and bulbs. Unfortunately many are made very cheaply – as are hand forks – and quickly bend or break, so buy a good strong one.

Rakes

There are a large number of different sizes and types of rake, all designed for different purposes.

The **wire**, **lawn** or **spring-tined rake** is sold for collecting debris off lawns or for scarifying – the process of vigorous raking of grass to remove moss and 'thatch'. It is excellent for the latter task but a plastic version is much better and easier to use for raking leaves and general use. Wire rakes are much better when used for raking gravel paths or for creating a very fine seed bed in preparation for sowing.

Plastic rakes come in a wide range of styles and are probably the best for general purpose work. They can be quite inexpensive to buy although those with extra-long (up to 1.8m) handles are usually more costly. These are worth the additional cost if you have a lot of regular raking to do for their length means that you can remain in an upright position: save your back by not extending the rake forwards as far as you can reach.

Traditional rakes are made of hardened steel and are used for raking soil level, clearing the surface of stones and firming seed beds or areas for turfing. Apart from a standard size, they also are available wider and with longer handle lengths. For levelling large areas of soil, some come with a raised back edge which simplifies the task.

Hoes

The garden hoe is a very useful tool for keeping borders weed free quickly – but only when used correctly. It is at its most effective when used before the weeds become too large and in dry, warm or windy conditions which makes the dislodged or cut growth shrivel before it can re-root. Keep the head of the hoe flat against or just below the soil surface and move back and forth. Remember to keep an eye out for any garden plant seedlings that you may want to keep and avoid hitting the stems of established garden plants.

Garden hoes come in several different head shapes, the most useful ones cutting on both the forward and backward motion. An occasional sharpening with a flat file can make a surprising difference to the tool's efficiency.

Patio knives

Not listed in many gardening books, this little hand tool with a thin 'L' shaped blade is perfect for the job it is designed for – getting weeds out of the cracks between paving slabs.

It is even better used as a mini hoe and hooking weeds out between plant stems providing you don't mind working on your hands and knees.

Cutting tools

Always buy the best quality cutting tools you can afford for there is nothing worse than having ones that don't cut cleanly or cannot be sharpened when necessary.

Secateurs

These are an essential piece of equipment for every gardener. Only use them for cutting plant material to keep the blade sharp and clean – if you need to cut string or anything else, use scissors.

Secateurs are available with two different cutting actions, anvil and standard. Anvil blades, where the top blade cuts down onto a flat, broad one can have a tendency to crush stems so you may find the standard type, which cut with a scissor action, better. Secateurs also can be bought with locking, telescopic handles which sound like a good idea but often come unlocked in use, which is irritating and may result in plant damage.

When cutting with secateurs it is important to cut cleanly. If you cannot cut the stem easily but find that you need to twist the secateurs you need to use **loppers** instead.

Loppers

Loppers are basically heavy duty secateurs with longer handles, especially useful when pruning shrubs and trees. All the notes referring to secateurs apply equally here. If you cannot cut the stem easily but find that you need to twist the loppers you need to use a **pruning saw**.

Pruning saws

The easiest ones to use are those with a curved blade for they enable it to get in amongst branches of trees and shrubs where an ordinary saw would have difficulty.

Pruning saws can be used on even quite large branches for their blades are very sharp. When cutting any branch support the weight of it if possible to prevent it from tearing away from the main stem which, apart from looking unsightly, may allow disease to enter. An easy alternative is to saw the branch off in sections so that the weight is less when it comes to the final cut.

Anything larger than a pruning saw can easily tackle, especially if it requires the use of a chainsaw, will need professional help.

Shears

A good pair of sharp garden shears is indispensable for cutting small areas of grass where mowers can't reach, although it would be more time efficient to invest in a strimmer or rethink the cutting regime – perhaps you could make this an area of longer grass only cut occasionally?

They are even more useful for the accurate cutting of topiary, small hedges and the unwanted growth of spent herbaceous plants.

For larger hedging, larger shears are available, often with a notch in the blade to cut through thicker stems although a powered hedge trimmer will be far more time effective.

Edging shears

Used solely for cutting lawn edges, they differ from ordinary shears in having long handles that allow the user to remain standing. If you have a lawn with flower borders cut into it then these are a must for nothing creates a better impression than a well cared for lawn. Cut the edges as often as need be, perhaps fortnightly. You can sometimes get away with not mowing the lawn if you run out of time providing you edge it – you'll be amazed by the trans-formation in its appearance.

If your lawn finishes flush against a path or other hard surface you will need to buy an **edging iron** which will create the same effect. This is sometimes referred to as a **half-moon** because of the shape of its single blade and is used by pushing it with your foot between the edge of the path and the lawn.

Power-driven tools

Whether powered by electricity or petrol these are likely to be amongst the most expensive purchases you make so it is important to work out exactly what you require them to do and not make costly mistakes.

Electric-powered tools have the advantage of being cleaner to use, instant – just flick a switch – and often quieter. However, apart from requiring a nearby power source which may be a problem in a larger garden, there are also additional safety considerations such as their use in wet conditions and having lengths of cables close to cutting blades. Before using electricity in the garden it is sensible to have your system checked by an electrician, perhaps having a RCD (residual current device) fitted which can detect some faults and automatically disconnect the supply.

Petrol-driven tools are more costly to purchase but are more powerful and have few of the limitations of electric. They will require regular servicing and there are the issues of storing petrol safely.

All power tools need to be used with care, taking special regard to the warnings relating to hearing and sight loss to both yourself and others nearby.

Mowers

Whether you have a tiny lawn or acres of grass to cut it is unlikely that you will want to resort to hand mowing with an old fashioned push mower. The sight of a well mown lawn always impresses and if the striped effect is a must for you then you need to remember that it is the roller on the mower and not the blades that create this – check that the mower has one fitted before buying.

Whether electric or petrol driven, there is a choice of cutting action – rotary or cylinder. Cylinder mowers are best avoided unless you have a perfectly level and well manicured lawn; they do not cut a weedy, damp or uneven surface well and the blades need to be kept sharp, a costly job best carried out by a specialist.

Rotary mowers, on the other hand, can cope with most types of grass, even long and unkempt, and some models will mow adequately when the grass is wet, an added bonus. It is usually easier and cheaper to replace the blades when they become blunt or damaged.

Another consideration is whether your mower needs a grass collection box. If you are able to mow the lawn very regularly it is possible to leave the clippings to disappear back into the lawn. The sight of cut grass strewn across the lawn will never give your garden the appearance you are striving for and so should be collected.

Is it more cost and time effective for you to pay someone to mow your grass rather than invest in expensive equipment? Many professional gardeners have their own mowers that they will bring with them.

Is the mower large enough or too large for the size of my garden? Is the grass box too small and so requires constant emptying? These are the questions that you need to ask yourself before buying. Specialist horticultural equipment suppliers often will have demonstration models that you can test at home before purchasing and it is certainly worth considering this to make sure that you are making the correct decisions.

For a quality cut always have the blades turning at full speed but travel slowly over the grass.

Strimmers

For cutting longer grass and rough areas, strimmers are ideal. Available powered by electric for light use in smaller gardens or more powerful petrol driven ones for larger areas, there is a knack to achieving an attractive finish which only comes with practice.

Avoid, at all costs, touching the base of trees for many are lost or irrevocably damaged by having their bark cut by the strimmer cord.

Strimmers are sometimes offered with steel blades for cutting woody stems. These need to be treated with extreme caution for the blade can shatter and full chainsaw safety clothing should always be worn.

Strimmers are one of those tools that attract attention and children are fascinated by them. Never use them when there are onlookers for debris can travel considerable distances at very high speeds and inflict severe injuries.

Hedge cutters

Just as with mowers or strimmers, hedge cutters can be powered by electricity or petrol. Special care must be taken with electric powered ones that the flex isn't cut – all too easy to do. Rechargeable battery operated models are available, some better and more efficient than others.

Hedge cutters are also available in different blade lengths but don't be tempted to buy the largest sizes just in the hope that you will finish the job more quickly. Always select by weight and balance for a heavy machine can make you very easily tire.

Leaf blowers

If you have a lot of deciduous trees in your garden or nearby you may prefer to use a leaf blower to help you collect their fallen leaves.

To be effective they need to be used correctly and it is not uncommon to see people being showered with the blown leaves as they struggle against the wind in a vain attempt to move them to a specific point. Always use the wind to assist with the moving of the leaves by blowing them into heaps before carrying them manually away.

There are both electric and petrol driven models – avoid those that are too bulky to use easily. Some blowers come with a collecting bag and a suction switch which can be useful on occasions, but often these have quite high vibration levels which can be damaging to nerves so only use for a short time. Backpack blowers, where the engine mountings are fitted to a back harness, are easy and comfortable to use even for longer periods. Leaf blowers are noisy so always make sure you wear ear defenders and goggles to protect your eyes from dust are also advisable.

Wheelbarrows, bags and sheets

A wheelbarrow can be useful for moving heavy loads or large quantities of waste material but do take up space storing.

Purpose-made bags or buckets can be bought but a free option is the large bags used by builder's merchants for moving gravel and sand. These can only be used once for that purpose so are easy to beg.

Sheets can also be bought with carrying handles in each corner and these are ideal for throwing garden waste onto especially if you are weeding on your hands and knees and a wheelbarrow is a bit high for comfort.

Regardless of which you use, don't be tempted to lift more weight than you can comfortably manage. By making frequent trips to the compost bins you are regularly changing your posture and helping to relax your muscles. Feeling tired after a hard day's work in the garden is natural; straining or injuring yourself is not.

Further Reading/Bibliography

The Royal Horticultural Society (RHS) produces numerous manuals both for the beginner and the more advanced. Their website www.rhs.org.uk is full of useful information on plants and techniques.

For organic gardening and composting look at Garden Organic: www.gardenorganic.org.uk

Compton, Tania and Lawson, Andrew, *Dream Gardens: 100 Inspirational Gardens*, London: Merrell, 2009.

Lloyd, Christopher, *Colour for Adventurous Gardeners*, London: BBC Books, 2001.

Verey, Rosemary, *Good Planting*, London: Frances Lincoln Publishers, 1990.

Verey, Rosemary, *The Making of a Garden*, London: Frances Lincoln Publishers, 2001.

Index